H O U R

of the

WITCH

Harry Potter,

Wicca Witchcraft,

and the Bible

HOUR
of the
WITCH

Harry Potter,

Wicca Witchcraft,

and the Bible

STEVE WOHLBERG

Destiny Image® **Publishers, Inc.**
P.O. Box 310
Shippensburg, PA 17257-0310

"Speaking to the Purposes of God for This Generation
and for the Generations to Come"

ISBN 0-7684-2279-5

For Worldwide Distribution
Printed in the U.S.A.

This book and all other Destiny Image, Revival Press, MercyPlace, Fresh Bread, Destiny Image Fiction, and Treasure House books are available at Christian bookstores and distributors worldwide.

1 2 3 4 5 6 7 8 9 10 / 10 09 08 07 06 05

For a U.S. bookstore nearest you, call **1-800-722-6774**.
For more information on foreign distributors, call **717-532-3040**.
Or reach us on the Internet:
www.destinyimage.com

Dedication

To Seth,
Love always, Dad

Contents

Foreword

Steve Wohlberg has glimpsed the horizon and issued an urgent warning.

Almost imperceptibly, an occult awakening began taking place in the shadows of the 1960s. Recently, it has exploded into a full-scale revival. "This isn't fantasy or fiction, but reality," Wohlberg says. "Make no mistake about it: Real witchcraft is here and it's not going away."

With fresh insight, *Hour of the Witch* looks at this Wiccan explosion—so foreign to so many. Its parallel focus is to examine one of the most telling signs of the occult revival, the *Harry Potter* phenomenon. He supplies background information that makes sense to the average reader and proves that *Harry Potter* is indeed fanning the flames of today's postmodern dalliance with Wicca and Neo-paganism.

We discover key facts that have eluded most commentaries, reviews, and warnings—even the little-known detail that while *Harry Potter* author J.K. Rowling was on a London train, the character of Harry Potter invaded her mind like a familiar spirit that had been summoned—and it happened in a split second, quicker than an elevator ride. Soon after this, Rowling began writing her long series of *Harry Potter* books. Little did she or anyone else know the extent that her Wiccan tales would invade the public forum, especially the youth culture.

There are things not always seen clearly. For instance, Wohlberg cites how the entire *Harry Potter* series is permeated with references to real-life, non-fiction places, persons, and common occult practices. Rowling did her homework. A good author does not write about witchcraft and the occult without researching it, perhaps even trying it out. In the end, the author often becomes an occult proponent, sharing the flavor and feel of this alien world with the fascinated reader. The kids pick it up. Then they delve deeper into this new realm of mystery. Naturally, each *Harry Potter* book (or movie) release causes a feeding frenzy as new records are set and former sales are surpassed. It is an addictive phenomenon. Retailers know it.

The economic facts alone clearly show the extent of this Neopagan revival. Wohlberg cites many impressive signs, including that "when *Harry Potter and the Prisoner of Azkaban* was released on Friday, June 4, 2004, it conjured up $92.7 million worth of ticket sales, representing the second-best weekend opening of all time, just behind *Spiderman*."

And Rowling's fortune? "She can buy an entire fleet of jets, and any company besides. Her story is one of the most amazing 'rags to riches' tales of the 21st century."

Steve Wohlberg asks: "Could there be something more than mere literary magic fueling the success of Rowling's novels?" The answer could be stranger than fiction, as I myself learned during previous years traveling throughout India.[1] Terms like "the spirit of the age" take on new meaning after reading *Hour of the Witch*. So do the apostle Paul's warnings about unseen "powers and principalities." This is serious business.

Steve Wohlberg entreats the reader like a father beckoning his wayward son. He does it in a way that is clear, fresh, and insightful, addressing not only Christians but also the wider secular audience. We learn how great is the alternative—not a sorcerer or wizard, but the One who came to redeem a lost planet, the Man With Scars.

We suddenly glimpse how bright His light is.

Tal Brooke
President of Spiritual Counterfeits Project (www.scp-inc.org)
Author of *One World* and *Avatar of Night*

ENDNOTE

1. See Tal Brooke's, *Avatar of Night* (Berkeley, CA: End Run Publishing, 1999).

CHAPTER 1

THE TIMES:

Hour of the Witch

Wicca may, in fact, be the fastest
growing religious movement in the United States.
—Kimberly Winston, "The Witch Next Door"[1]

My wife Kristin and I noticed her immediately. We were sitting quietly in the lobby of a medical center in Templeton, California, waiting to see the doctor who was monitoring the progress of Kristin's pregnancy. Suddenly a mysterious looking young lady— probably in her twenties—entered and sat directly in front of us. She had long dark hair, was dressed in black (which seemed slightly unusual for a spring day in May), and began reading a book with a full moon on the cover. When the nurse called out, "Kristin Wohlberg," and we rose to leave the room, I glanced once more and noticed she was wearing a necklace with a five-pointed star, or pentagram. Was she a practicing witch? I can't say for sure, but on the surface, the signs certainly fit.

In case you haven't noticed, Wicca witchcraft—also called "the Craft"—is growing rapidly throughout the United States, Canada, and around the world. Referred to as the "Old Religion" by practitioners, researchers say it entered America in the 1960s when Raymond Buckland (a disciple of British occultist Gerald Gardner) first established a coven in New York.[2]

> Buckland's coven initiated others, who in turn began their own covens, and initiated still others… The "counterculture" of the middle and late sixties was perfectly timed to stimulate the slowly growing Wiccan movement. The counterculture's endorsement of drugs, sexual liberty, mysticism, enlightenment, self-divination, occultism, and anti-Christianity was tailor-made to encourage the explosive growth of neo-paganism, in general and neo-witchcraft in particular. The rest is history.[3]

Wicca's growth in the 1970s and 1980s remained steady, yet unspectacular, until the 1990s when the movement experienced a dramatic spike in numbers. In 1999, Craig Hawkins, author of *Witchcraft: Exploring the World of Wicca*, put the U.S. witch population somewhere around 200,000.[4] At the same time Phyllis Curott, nationally-known Wiccan High Priestess and best-selling author of *The Book of Shadows: A Modern Woman's Journey Into the Wisdom of Witchcraft and the Magic of the Goddess*, estimated the numbers as between 3 million and 5 million Wiccans in the United States alone.[5]

Regardless of who is correct—Hawkins or Curott—increasing numbers of witches are flying out of the broom closet. In 1998, the *Chicago Tribune* reported: "Neo-paganism is the fastest-growing religion in North America with the Internet being the prime means of proselytizing."[6] In 2001, the American Religious Identification Survey (ARIS), conducted by the Graduate Center of the City University of New York, indicated seventeen-fold growth in the Wiccan community between 1990 and 2001—the highest of any faith group monitored. "This would indicate a doubling in numbers of adherents about every 2.5 years."[7] Curott estimates faster growth, suggesting "a doubling of size every 18 months."[8] If either figure is accurate and if this trend continues, "Wicca [could] be the third largest religious group in the U.S. by about 2012, behind Christianity and Judaism."[9]

Adults aren't the only ones interested in the Craft; kids are too. A 2004 article in *ReligionLink* (a resource for news reporters) entitled, "Wicca Moves Into the Mainstream," says, "Wicca has enchanted pop culture and many teenagers...."[10] In fact, so many teenagers have recently embraced the Wiccan way that in 2004 even National Public Radio's *All Things Considered* aired a story called "Teens and Wicca" informing the American public that more kids than parents realize hide spell books under their beds, visit popular witchcraft web sites, keep in touch with other Craft-exploring kids through email and the Internet, and meet in small groups called "covens" to practice magic.[11]

Why the explosion of interest—especially among teenagers—in witchcraft and casting spells? One reason is clear: In the last few years both children and adults have been exposed to a vast array of pleasantly designed books, supernaturally charged TV programs, and magical movies portraying witchcraft as safe, exciting, and spiritually empowering—especially for teenage girls. The most popular TV shows and films of this type include:

- *The Witches of Eastwick* (Movie, 1987): Three restless women in a sleepy New England village "turn to witchcraft for entertainment."[12]

- *The Craft* (Movie, 1996): Enticingly depicts the adventures of "a coven of witches who are still in high school."[13]

- *Practical Magic* (Movie, 1998): Sandra Bullock and Nicole Kidman star as two witches. "Raised by their aunts after their parents' death, the sisters grew up in a household that was anything but typical. The little girls ate chocolate cake for breakfast, stayed up late and studied spell books, practicing the ancient arts of white magic that had been handed down through their family from generation to generation."[14]

- ***Sabrina, the Teenage Witch*** (TV series): About a "girl with supernatural powers" who learns "to use her witch-craft wisely."[15]

- ***Buffy the Vampire Slayer*** (TV series): Starring a blonde teenager who battles vampires, monsters, and other creatures of the night. Buffy's friend Willow, nicknamed "The Willow Witch," reveals positive "interest and involvement in Wicca and Witchcraft."[16]

- ***Charmed*** (TV series): Features three sexy sorceress sisters who "use their individual powers as good witches to battle the forces of evil."[17]

The popularity of these mesmerizing shows has made this fact obvious: sorcery sells. As a result, even respectable children's book publishers have capitalized on the current craze-for-the-Craft by introducing a steady stream of witchcraft novels just for kids and teenagers. Some of the most profitable series include:

- ***The W.I.T.C.H*** series (Hyperion): Launched into America in April 2004 with ads funded by The Walt Disney Company, this internationally popular series follows the journeys of "five ordinary girls just going into their teens" who have "super powers over the Elements."[18]

- ***The Daughters of the Moon*** series, by Lynne Ewing (Hyperion): "About a group of girls in L.A. None of these girls are normal, each has a secret power which makes them different."[19] Book titles include: *Goddess of the Night*, *The Sacrifice*, and *Possession*.

- ***The Sweep*** series, by Cate Tiernan (Penguin Putnam Books for Young Readers): Perhaps the most gruesome and violent sequence of witchcraft tales for kids. Book titles include: *Blood Witch*, *Dark Magick*, and *Spellbound*.

Moving beyond Hollywood productions and fictitious novels, occult publishers are also capitalizing on the effects of movies and novels by churning out a growing body of how-to-practice-the-real-thing non-fiction works. Advertising dollars are netting results, and sales are soaring. The following is just a tiny sample of books written by practicing witches that are now easily available at Barnes & Noble bookstores, on Amazon.com, or even Walmart.com:

- **Teen Witch: Wicca for a New Generation**, by Silver Ravenwolf (Llewellyn Publications, 1997): Interviewed by *The New York Times* as a Wiccan expert, Ravenwolf has produced an entire line of Witchcraft 101 books for searching teens. "One of the most famous witches in the world today,"[20] her many works include, *To Ride a Silver Broomstick*, *To Stir a Magick Cauldron*, *Silver's Spells for Prosperity*, and *Teen Witch Kit*, which has "everything the novice spell caster needs to practice the Craft."[21]

- **Llewellyn's Teen Witch Datebook** (Llewellyn Publications, 2004): Because "Teens everywhere are coming out of the broom closet, hungry for information and tools to aid them in their spiritual quest," *Datebook* offers "dozens of rituals, and articles by well-known Pagan writers."[22]

- **21st Century Wicca: A Young Witch's Guide to Living the Magical Life**, by Jennifer Hunter (Citadel Press, 1997).

- **A Charmed Life: Celebrating Wicca Every Day**, by Patricia J. Telesco (New Page Books, 2000).

- **Sons of the Goddess: A Young Man's Guide to Wicca**, by Christopher Penczak (Llewellyn Publication, 2005).

- **Empowering Your Life With Wicca**, by Sirona Knight (Alpha Books, 2003).

- **Wicca for Couples: Making Magic Together**, by A.J. Drew (New Page Books, 2002).

The list is endless. There are also witchcraft games, such as C.J. Carella's *Witchcraft Role Playing Game*, "a game of modern magic and dark secrets;"[23] and magazines, like *Witchcraft & Wicca*, published bi-yearly by The Children of Artemis;[24] and international events, such as *Witchfest International*, held November 2004 in London. Proclaimed as "the largest witchcraft festival in the world within recorded history,"[25] Witchfest featured professional entertainment (Mediaeval Baebes, Daughters of Elvin, etc.), plus lectures and workshops by some of the world's most famous Wiccan authors. To meet growing demands for all things witchy, Mattel Toys now sells a Secret Spells Barbie doll, complete with witch costume, cauldron, and magic powder. There's even a *Wicca and Witchcraft for Dummies* book (John Wiley & Sons Inc., 2005), making sorcery super simple for the average Joe.

This isn't fantasy or fiction, but reality. Make no mistake about it: Witchcraft is here and it's not going away. Movies, TV shows, games, toys, magazines, books, and web sites are now taking full advantage of the interest and dollars of youth and adults. If you doubt the trend, just go to the Internet web site: www.walmart.com and type "Wicca" into the search field. You'll be shocked. One book listed is entitled, *Rocking the Goddess: Campus Wicca for the Student Practitioner*, by Anthony Paige (Citadel Press, 2002). Wal-Mart's own web site declares:

> Written by a student for students, Rocking the Goddess is the first book of its kind for the budding Wiccan. Included here are interviews with students, faculty, and college administrators across the country, as well as profiles of Wiccan role models such as Enya, Stevie Nicks, and Tori Amos.[26]

Witchcraft is growing so fast on high school and college campuses that Wiccan visionaries are rushing to establish their own schools. "The growth has been so explosive that what structure there is cannot accommodate it," says Chas Clifton, editor of *Pomegranate: The International Journal of Pagan Studies*. "We are like a third world country that can't put up enough elementary schools fast enough...."[27] It seems a sorcery-filled tsunami is forming—with no stopping it.

Yet when it comes to this surging current, there's one sequence of books and films that tower above all others in popularity and controversy.

They're loved and hated, praised and feared, considered innocuous or full of subtle dangers. You know the name: *Harry Potter*.

Most parents see the *Harry Potter* novels written by Joanne Kathleen Rowling as harmless entertainment not worth worrying about. They surely don't see any subtle (or dangerous) Harry–Wicca connection. Others do; in fact, many are certain that dark spiritual forces lurk beneath those magic-made-funny pages. Are J.K. Rowling's best-selling books (even if this isn't her conscious intent) fueling teenage interest in the Craft? "Don't be silly!" shout Potter supporters. "Open your eyes!" counter Potter critics. Which side is right?

What if *Harry Potter* is fanning a witchy flame, so what? What's the problem? What is Wicca witchcraft all about anyway, and why are so many searching youth and adults exploring its mysteries? Wicca claims to be a valid pathway to spiritual enlightenment—simply a gentle nature religion peacefully tapping into Earth's natural energies and seasons. Is it really? Or is it inherently a dangerous movement, capable of deceiving and even harming its own practitioners?

One reason why *Harry Potter* is considered beneficial to youth is because of its apparent portrayal of humanity's classic struggle between "good and evil." Yet significantly, the same kind of struggle is not only depicted in the fictitious *Charmed, W.I.T.C.H., Sweep*, and *Daughters of the Moon* novels, but also in the non-fiction works of Phyllis Curott, Silver Ravenwolf, Jennifer Hunter, Patricia Telesco, Sirona Knight, and countless other Wiccan authors. They *all* describe an ongoing battle between good and evil, of right against wrong. And of course, each claims to promote goodness. Because the *Potter* books and movies do the same thing, this enhances the almost universal belief that they're conveyors of positive moral principles and are appropriate entertainment for our sons and daughters.

These questions are worth considering: What really is "good" and "evil"? Are there white witches and dark ones, like Wiccans claim and as *Harry Potter* describes? What about witchcraft itself? Is it a neutral science, capable of being used for good or evil depending upon the intent of the practitioner? Is there any objective standard to help us discern the difference between right and wrong, or should we simply follow what looks, sounds, seems, or feels right to our families, friends, society, or our own hearts? And what about the oft-overlooked reality that absolute evil can be highly intelligent, purposefully subtle, can hide itself, and can even masquerade as something positive? This book will explore and answer these questions, and many more.

Welcome to *Hour of the Witch*.

Prepare yourself for a fascinating journey into a mysterious subject. You'll be amazed at what you find.

ENDNOTES

1. Article entitled, "The Witch Next Door," by Kimberly Winston, November 11, 2004. See http://www.beliefnet.com/story/155/story_15517.html.

2. *Spiritual Counterfeits Project Journal*, Vol. 16:3, 1991. "Witchcraft: From the Dark Ages to the New Age." A Special Report by Brooks Alexander, p. 34.

3. *Ibid.*, p. 35.

4. Catherine Edwards, "Wicca Casts Spell on Teen-Age Girls," quoted in *Insight* online magazine, Vol. 15, No. 39, October 25, 1999. Published date: October 1, 1999 (Washington, D.C.).

5. *Ibid.*

6. Quoted in: "21st Century Challenges to Separation of Religion and Government," Jefferson 21st Century Institute, at: http://www.j21c.org/challeng.htm.

7. "American Religious Identification Survey," by The Graduate Center of the City University of New York, at: http://www.gc.cuny.edu/studies/.

8. *Wicca: World View Summary* by Amanda Tippy & Dr. Ray Lubeck. Reported on http://www.multnomah.edu/Worldseen/Wicca.html.

9. *Ibid.*

10. ReligionLink, "Wicca Moves Into the Mainstream," October 11, 2004. See http://www.religionlink.org/tip_041011azones.php.

11. National Public Radio's *All Things Considered*, report by Barbara Bradley Hagerty: "New Religion in America: Alternative Movements Gain Ground with Flexibility, Modernity...Part 4: Teens and Wicca." May 13, 2004. See http://www.npr.org/templates/story/story.php?storyId=1895496.

12. See http://www.witchcraft.org/video/eastwick.htm.

13. See http://www.witchcraft.org/video/craft.htm.

14. See http://www.witchcraft.org/video/practical.htm.

15. Described on Yahoo TV: See http://tv.yahoo.com/tvpdb?id=1807777356&d=tvi&cf=0.

16. See http://www.witchcraft.org/video/buffy.htm.

17. See http://www.witchcraft.org/video/charmed.htm and http://www.tvtome.com/Charmed/ (official web site).

18 See http://disney.go.com/witch/main.html.

19. See http://www.geocities.com/daughters_ofthe_moon/.

20. Silver Ravenwolf, *Teen Witch: Wicca for a New Generation* (St. Paul, MN: Llewellyn Publications, 2003), p. xiii.

21. *Ibid.*, Advertisement at the back of the book.

22. *Ibid.*, Advertisement at the back of the book.

23. See http://www.edenstudios.net/witchcraft/4000HC.html.

24. See http://www.witchcraft.org.

25. *Ibid.*, as of September 26, 2004; See also http://www.witchfest.net.

26. See http://www.walmart.com, search for *Rocking the Goddess: Campus Wicca for the Student Practitioner* by Anthony Paige (Citadel Press, 2002).

27. Winston, "The Witch Next Door."

CHAPTER 2

THE CRAZE:
Pottermania

J.K. Rowling has mesmerized an entire generation of kids.
—TIME Magazine[1]

It all began on a seemingly normal day in 1990 as a 25-year-old woman and wanna-be writer named Joanne Kathleen Rowling was traveling by train on the outskirts of London. As the train meandered peacefully through the pleasant British countryside, suddenly—like a revelation out of nowhere—Joanne saw "very, very clearly" the crystal-clear image of "Harry" as he popped into her mind. "The character of Harry just strolled into my head...I really did feel he was someone who walked up and introduced himself in my mind's eye."[2] With fascinated interest, she beheld an odd-looking, dark-haired boy wearing large spectacles. Somehow she imagined this kid was a wizard who didn't know he was a wizard. After pondering the idea, Rowling soon began working on a manuscript destined to form the basis of "the most popular children's series ever written."[3]

After her marriage ended in divorce, Rowling worked periodically on her book during the next few years, sometimes in coffee shops, or at home, while her little daughter Jessica napped. Financially poor and living on welfare, she struggled daily to make ends meet. After submitting her work to various publishers who only fired back rejection letters, Rowling finally received exciting news: *Harry Potter and the Philosopher's Stone* was accepted for publication by Scholastic, Inc. The title was later changed to *Harry Potter and the Sorcerer's Stone* for an American audience. Fifty thousand copies were printed in September of 1998. Unexpectedly, sales exploded.

The next volume (number two in a seven-part series), *Harry Potter and the Chamber of Secrets*, broke out in June 1999 with an initial printing of 250,000 books, five times more than *Sorcerer's Stone*. A mere three months later (September 1999), the printer cranked out 500,000 copies of *Harry Potter and the Prisoner of Azkaban*. By the summer of 2000, the first three *Harry Potter* books had grossed approximately $480 million, with over 35 million copies in print in 35 languages. In the publishing world, such sales were unprecedented.

The fourth title, *Harry Potter and the Goblet of Fire* (July 2000), became "the fastest selling book in history."[4] Its initial run was 5.3 million copies, with the majority entering eager hands in only one weekend, an all-time publishing record. Believe it or not, this was easily topped by the fifth installment, *Harry Potter and the Order of the Phoenix* (June 2003), which Scholastic, Inc. rolled out to the profitable tune of 8.5 million books. Over 250 million *Harry Potter* books have sold in over 200 countries and 60 languages, with two more books looming on the horizon. How big will Pottermania get? Only God knows.

Here are a few more facts:

- In June of 1999, *Harry Potter and the Sorcerer's Stone* became Number One on *The New York Times*, *Wall Street Journal*, and *USA Today* best-seller lists—all at the same time.[5] By September, book three was not only Number One on *The Wall Street Journal* list, but books one and two carried the Number Two and Number Three slots, a first in U.S. publishing history.

THE CRAZE: **Pottermania**

- The legendary Warner Brothers, Inc., has committed to producing seven full-length *Harry Potter* movies to coincide with each of the seven books. In 2001, *Harry Potter and the Sorcerer's Stone* (film one) opened with $90.3 million; in 2002, *Harry Potter and the Chamber of Secrets* (film two) débuted wtih $88.4 million.[6] When *Harry Potter and the Prisoner of Azkaban* was released on Friday, June 4, 2004, it conjured up $92.7 million worth of ticket sales in North America alone, representing the second-best weekend opening of all time, just behind *Spiderman*.[7] Production of the fourth film is now in progress.

- Before the release of *Harry Potter and the Order of the Phoenix* (book five), Amazon received advance payments for 1.3 million copies.[8] Barnes & Noble also sold 896,000 copies in one day. "It's unstoppable," reported Steve Riggio, the chief CEO of Barnes & Noble.[9]

- *Harry Potter* books have not only been incorporated into the United States public school curriculum (with teacher's manuals and discussion guides), but they've also spawned a multi-million-dollar line of Potter merchandise, which includes games, puzzles, posters, toys, clocks, shirts, hats, costumes, eyeglasses, towels, blankets, playing cards, markers, pens, lunch boxes, mugs, bookmarks, jelly beans, stamps, and much more.

When *Harry Potter and the Goblet of Fire* first hit bookstores:

Nightfall on July 7, 2000 found both children and adults waiting in long lines to obtain a copy of Rowling's work. *The New York Times* reported that the onslaught of excited children "created bedlam at bookstores." Children were crying, store clerks were cursing, and numerous scuffles broke out between enraged customers wrestling over the last remaining copies. Bay Anapol, the *Harry Potter* party organizer for a bookstore in Santa Fe, New Mexico, described it very well:

"It's that cabbage patch doll mentality all over again. People have been calling panic-stricken over not being able to get a book."

At one store in England, where J.K. Rowling appeared, police had to be called in to control the mayhem that included fathers fighting to secure a closer spot from which to view Rowling. A similar situation arose at a Borders store in New Jersey when Rowling showed up in October of 1999 to promote her third book, *Harry Potter and the Prisoner of Azkaban*. Police were summoned when the estimated crowd of 2,000 became unruly and practically rioted because Rowling had to leave early. "It was a total fiasco, really ugly," said Matthew Demakos, who witnessed the scene. "Irate parents were screaming; people who had bought books were demanding their money back." The store's manager was reportedly "bitten and punched" by angry *Potter* fans.[10]

Researcher, author, and cult expert Richard Abanes, whose dozen-plus books have brought him national recognition, summarized the scene in his best-selling book, *Harry Potter and the Bible: The Menace Behind the Magick*:

> The release of J.K. Rowling's fourth novel, *Harry Potter and the Goblet of Fire*, created a worldwide wave of consumerism hysteria the likes of which had never before been seen in the book-buying community.[11]

Needless to say, Joanne Kathleen Rowling isn't on welfare anymore. She's remarried and is now one of the world's richest women, even wealthier than England's Queen. She doesn't need to travel by train either, but has enough money in the bank to hire a private jet to take her anywhere she wants to go. Forget "hire." She can *buy* an entire fleet of jets, and any company besides. Her story is one of the most amazing "rags to riches" tales of the 21st century.

What is *Harry Potter* all about anyway? In the next chapter we'll look at its basic story line, reveal some interesting details, and later delve deeper by exploring the battle raging between *Potter* fans and foes over whether Pottermania is just harmless fantasy, not worth thinking twice about, or whether it contains subtle and dangerous elements now sneaking under society's radar screen.

Jean Feiwel, a representative of Rowling's publisher, scratched her head, saying:

> It's mind-boggling. It would be easy to attribute *Harry Potter's* success to some form of magical intervention.[12]

Richard Abanes agrees, yet he questions the nature of the magical intervention lurking behind *Harry's* enchanting influence. In his book, *Harry Potter and the Bible*, Abanes asks these probing questions:

> Is the success behind Rowling's books just a result of good writing and media hype? Or is there an unseen spiritual force of darkness possibly driving the craze?[13]

Is the latter possible? In other words, could there be something more than mere literary magic fueling the success of Rowling's novels? Something more akin to a *real spell* cast by some sinister source? If there is, wouldn't it be wise to become knowledgeable about the nature and agenda of this unseen influence? Yes, it would.

Let's try to find out if there is indeed a hidden menace beneath the magic.

As we delve deeper, don't forget—Harry Potter *is* a sorcerer.

ENDNOTES

1. *TIME Magazine,* June 23, 2003, p. 6.

2. Richard Abanes, *Harry Potter and the Bible: The Menace Behind the Magick* (Camp Hill, PA: Horizon Books, 2001), p. 21. J.K. Rowling quoted in Reuters, "Harry Potter 'Strolled Into My Head,'" July 17, 2000.

3. *TIME Magazine*, June 23, 2003, p. 63.

4. *Newsweek*, June 30, 2003, p. 52.

5. *Harry Potter and the Chamber of Secrets*, Final Production Information (Warner Brothers). See http://movies.warnerbros.com/pub/movie/potter2/potter2notes.htm.

6. Internet Movie Database statistics, "News for Harry Potter and the Chamber of Secrets." See http://us.imdb.com/title/tt0295297/news.

7. John Hamaan, "Potter Takes Box Office Prisoner" (June 6, 2004). See http://www.boxofficeprophets.com/column/index.cfm?columnID=8381.

8. Jacqueline Blais, "Harry Potter Casts a Record-Breaking Spell," *USA Today* (June 22, 2003). See http://www.usatoday.com/life/books/news/2003-06-22-potter-main_x.htm.

9. *Ibid.*

10. Abanes, *Harry Potter and the Bible*, pp. 204-205. Sources: David D. Kirkpatrick, "Harry Potter Magic Halts Bedtime for Youngsters," *New York Times*, July 9, 2000, available at www.cesnur.org/recens/potter_036.htm; Bay Anapol, quoted in Kirkpatrick; Amelia Hill, "Harry Potter and the Small Snubbed Fans," *The Observer* (London), July 9, 2000, available online at www.observer.co.uk; Shannon Maughan, "Keeping Up With Harry," *Publishers Weekly*, November 1, 1999, available online at www.publishersweekly.com/articles/19991101_82411.asp.

11. Abanes, *Harry Potter and the Bible*, p. 203.

12. *Ibid.*, p. 2. Elizabeth Mehren, "Despite Sales, Some Not Wild About Harry Potter Books," *Los Angeles Times*, October 22, 1999, available online at www.latimes.com.

13. *Ibid.*, p. 6.

CHAPTER 3

THE STORY:

Harry Potter Goes to Hogwarts

It is good to see that the best selling series
of books in the Western world is such
a positive tale about witches and wizards.
—The Children of Artemis
(a Witchcraft & Wicca web site)[1]

J.K. Rowling's *Harry Potter* books are a highly imaginative series of fantasy novels chronicling the adventures of an orphan boy named Harry Potter whose parents, James and Lily Potter (a wizard and a witch), were brutally murdered by "the greatest Dark sorcerer of all time, Lord Voldemort," when Harry was one year old.[2] After pulverizing James and Lily with a deadly burst of greenish light, Mr. Wicked tried to kill baby Harry too, but somehow the toddler survived—as a result of his mother's love—his only wound being a lightning-shaped scar seared into his forehead when Voldemort's death-curse unexplainably bounced back on himself, stripping him of his powers and even his physical body. Critically injured, the Dark One faded mysteriously into the night.

Shortly after the horrible death of Harry Potter's parents (who were greatly loved in the wizard world), Albus Dumbledore, the Headmaster of the prestigious 1000-year-old Hogwarts School of Witchcraft and Wizardry, leaves baby Harry inside a basket on the doorstep of Harry's non-magical relatives, the Dursley family, with a note in his tiny hand explaining what happened and urging them to take the boy in. Reluctantly (for they detest everything magical), the Dursleys accept the responsibility and raise Harry Potter, but never reveal to him the contents of the letter.

Harry has an awful childhood. The Dursleys despise him, forcing him to sleep in a dusty closet under the stairs. On Harry's 11th birthday, the family receives an unexpected and rather frightening visit from Hagrid, the Keeper of the Keys at Hogwarts, who is sent by Headmaster Dumbledore to inform Harry Potter that he should now prepare for his first semester at sorcery school, which will begin very soon. To Harry's utter amazement, Hagrid tells him what happened to his parents (this is the first Harry learns of it), then informs him that he's really a wizard and is even famous throughout the world of witches and sorcerers as the only one to have survived an assault from "He-Who-Cannot-Be-Named."

Hagrid hands Harry a letter, which reads:

HOGWARTS SCHOOL *of* WITCHCRAFT *and* WIZARDRY
Headmaster: ALBUS DUMBLEDORE
(Order of Merlin, First Class, Grand Sorc., Chf. Warlock,
Supreme Mugwump, International Federation of Wizards)

Dear Mr. Potter,

We are pleased to inform you that you have been accepted at Hogwarts School of Witchcraft and Wizardry. Please find enclosed a list of all necessary books and equipment.

Term begins on September 1. We await your owl [wizards send messages back and forth via owls] by no later than July 31.

Yours sincerely,
Minerva McGonagall,
Deputy Headmistress[3]

THE STORY: **Harry Potter Goes to Hogwarts**

I'm leaving the Dursleys! Harry realizes. His emotions surge as he happily packs his bags for Hogwarts to begin a new, adventurous, and thrills-packed life. Yet, detailed instructions must be followed. Before going to Hogwarts, Harry is told he must first visit Diagon Alley inside of London (an alley invisible except to wizard-eyes) where he must purchase a list of required textbooks, a wand, a cauldron (for mixing potions), a telescope (for studying astrology), and other sorcery-related necessities.

Harry's list of textbooks include:

A History of Magic by Bathilda Bagshot
The Standard Book of Spells (Grade 1)
Magical Theory by Adalbert Waffling
Magical Drafts and Potions by Arsenius Jigger
The Dark Forces: A Guide to Self-Protection by Quentin
    Trimble[4]
"Can we buy all these in London?" Harry wondered aloud.
"If yeh know where to go," said Hagrid.[5]

Hogwarts is located outside of London in sort of a parallel-to-this-world dimension, not easily observed and invisible to most. To get there, Harry Potter is instructed by Hagrid that he must first go to the King's Cross subway station in London (this station exists in real life) and walk through a solid wall that separates platform nine and platform ten, so he can miraculously emerge onto platform nine and three-quarters—a platform visible only to the enlightened eyes of wizards. Hoping against hope that Hagrid's instructions will work, Harry plunges straight into the barrier, passes through unharmed, and suddenly finds himself standing before a scarlet steam engine on platform nine and three-quarters surrounded by scores of excited young witches and wizards with their parents. "Hogwarts Express, eleven o'clock," flashes a sign above the train.

Hogwarts School of Witchcraft and Wizardry is a mystical training school filled with secret chambers, hidden passages, and dark corridors where students, ages 11 to 17, study the ancient art of sorcery.

Students stay in four dormitories (Gryffindor, Hufflepuff, Ravenclaw, or Slytherin), eat meals in the Great Hall, do homework assignments in the library (except in the Restricted Section, which contains books on Black Magic), and take these required classes: History of Magic, Divination, Charms, Herbology, Care of Magical Creatures, Potions, Transfiguration, and Defense Against the Dark Arts. Just like real kids in regular schools, Hogwarts' boys and girls also take quizzes, tests, mid-term evaluations, and final exams—the most important being their O.W.L.s (Ordinary Wizarding Levels) given to fifth-year students. Achieving a high score on an O.W.L. greatly improves a graduate's chance of getting a better job working for grown-up sorcerers.

As a student, Harry Potter develops friendships with other young wizards and witches, especially Ron Weasley and Hermione Granger. Throughout the fantasy novels (and this constitutes no small part of their appeal to young readers), the author effectively weaves in many relational dynamics and issues so common today among typical teens, such as peer rivalry, lack of interest in homework, the fun of dorm life, off-campus school trips, the challenge of inter-dorm sporting events, the thrill of victory, the agony of defeat, attraction to the opposite sex, jealousies, fits of anger, embarrassment, hurt feelings, loneliness, and estranged friends making up. Thus, this incredibly popular story line includes many basic feelings, experiences, and activities common among kids and teenagers everywhere—whether in real-life elementary, middle, and high schools, or inside the fictitious Hogwarts School of Witchcraft and Wizardry. Mrs. Rowling *is* a good writer.

Harry Potter books also show no lack of humor (not all in good taste), and contain large amounts of just plain goofiness, being filled with scenes where spells backfire, sending students to the sick ward, magical bubble-gum pranks cause faces to swell, tails sprout behind kids' buttocks, quirky house elves say dumb things, boys vomit snails, and a stuffy news reporter turns into a beetle.

Beyond the humor and silliness are the highly imaginative and extremely frightening portrayals of Lord Voldemort's steady return to power, his deadly appearances both outside and inside of Hogwarts, and the ongoing struggle with this monstrously sinister warlock and his devoted followers (called Death Eaters) who perform dark spells against Harry Potter, his school-age friends, and Albus Dumbledore, the much-esteemed Headmaster of Hogwarts. These vivid depictions give many young readers nightmares.

Almost every *Harry Potter* book opens with Harry aimlessly spending the latter part of the summer months with the Dursley family. A unique plot unfolds, then each story progresses with Harry entering London, passing through the barrier at the King's Cross subway station, riding the Hogwarts Express, and then meandering through another action-packed school year at sorcery school. Each volume also contains some sort of scary encounter between Harry Potter and Lord Voldemort, which winds up with Albus Dumbledore teaching some new lesson to Harry, and finally concludes with a wiser and more-experienced wizard-boy reluctantly returning to an extremely boring, non-magical life with the cranky Dursley family at the end of each school year.

That's the gist of *Harry Potter*—at least on the surface. Right now, all over Planet Earth, on every continent around the globe, literally millions of young readers can hardly wait for the release of the next eerie book or mesmerizing movie, as the captivating drama follows the development of Harry Potter's magical abilities and rolls relentlessly onward toward some sort of edge-of-your-seat, blood-curdling showdown between the orphaned wizard-kid and Mr. Blackness himself, who is determined to regain his lost powers, recover his dissipated body, finish Harry off, and dominate the entire wizard world.

Again, we've only scratched the surface. As we shall soon see, the deeper we delve into *Harry Potter and the Sorcerer's Stone*, *Harry Potter and the Chamber of Secrets*, *Harry Potter and the Prisoner of Azkaban*, *Harry Potter and the Goblet of Fire*, *Harry Potter and the Order of the Phoenix*, or *Harry Potter and the Half-Blood Prince*, the more clearly we see that J.K. Rowling's imaginative story line, intricate details, and occult connections—as well as the issues involving the highly susceptible minds of boys and girls—are far from simple.

Next we will look at the heated controversy (both pro and con) surrounding these incredibly popular novels and films. Beyond this, we'll explore other significant details in Rowling's best-selling tale—details linked to *real* witchcraft, its history and philosophy, and details about the character of Albus Dumbledore himself, the Headmaster of Hogwarts, a man so skilled in the techniques of sorcery that he sometimes "radiates an indefinable sense of power"[6] unknown to mere mortals.

And we'll do it in the illuminating light of another best-selling Book—not *Harry Potter*, but the Holy Bible.

ENDNOTES

1. As of September 17, 2004, this quote was found on http://www.witchcraft.org/pastnews.html. Quoted by Richard Abanes, in *Harry Potter and the Bible: The Menace Behind the Magick* (Camp Hill, PA: Horizon Books, 2001), p. 13.

2. Rowling, *Chamber of Secrets*, p. 4.

3. Rowling, *Sorcerer's Stone*, p. 51.

4. Rowling, *Sorcerer's Stone*, p. 66.

5. Rowling, *Sorcerer's Stone*, p. 67.

6. Rowling, *Goblet of Fire*, p. 706.

CHAPTER 4

THE CONTROVERSY:
Is Harry Healthy for Kids?

The ultimate measure of a man is not where
he stands in moments of comfort and convenience, but where
he stands at times of challenge and controversy.
—Martin Luther King, Jr. (1929-1964)
American Civil Rights Leader

B ased on the incredible popularity of the *Harry Potter* series—not
only in North America but around the world—it seems rather obvious that the vast majority of parents and educators view the entire
Potter phenomenon as simply wonderful, completely harmless, magi-
cally wholesome, and exciting besides. If they didn't, they certainly
wouldn't allow their precious sons, daughters, and students to read
("devour" fits better) the books or munch on popcorn while watching
the movies. Sellers of *Potter* merchandise aren't complaining either. To
most, especially the kids, Joanne Kathleen Rowling is a modern hero-
ine; a lady who has conquered the odds, achieved success, and lavished
upon humanity a classic series of creative literature. The media largely
shares this view as well. Sinister? Dangerous? Don't be silly.

In addition to the belief that *Harry Potter* is good ol' fashioned fun, there are five main arguments now being used by supportive parents and teachers in favor of J.K. Rowling's series:

1. *Harry Potter* has achieved the unbelievable feat of motivating almost an entire generation of 21st century, media-saturated, video-game-addicted kids to actually turn off the TV and *read books*—which *must* be a good thing, right?

2. *Harry Potter* models the importance of developing loyal friendships with peers, such as those formed between Harry Potter, Ron Weasley, and Hermione Granger, as they work together against Lord Voldemort and his slimy Death Eaters.

3. *Harry Potter* contains timeless insights into the classic struggle between good and evil, and includes valuable moral lessons. This is the primary reason why the novels are being used in the United States public school system and why even some teachers have decorated their classrooms Hogwarts-style.

4. *Harry Potter* aids the development of children's imagination.

5. *Harry Potter* is entirely fictitious. All references to witchcraft and sorcery are mere literary devices with no connection to real occultism.

Although these arguments express today's majority opinion, not everyone agrees, and significantly, the dissent is quite sizable. On the opposite side of the fence, these highly concerned individuals—which also include many parents and teachers—don't want their kids reading *Harry Potter* at all. They don't think the series is wholesome fare, and they strongly oppose exposing the minds of their sons and daughters to *Harry* in the classroom. In fact, *Potter* protesters in the United States pack so much punch that *TIME Magazine* reported frankly:

Not all the numbers are nice, of course: the American Library Association ranks the *Harry Potter* books as the most challenged in the country; more parents have requested that *Harry Potter* be banished from bookshelves than they have *Huck Finn*, more than *Catcher in the Rye*.[1]

"The most challenged in the country" and "banished from bookshelves" aren't minor sentences. A fierce debate is raging! And with the release of every new *Harry Potter* book or movie, sparks fly in homes, on the radio, on the Net, on elementary, middle school, and high school campuses, within parent-teacher conferences, and in the national media. The intense controversy is even churning inside churches and between well-respected Christian leaders.

While many Christians oppose *Harry*, other Christians believe J.K. Rowling's books are beneficial and uplifting. For example, author Connie Neal's book, *What's a Christian to Do With Harry Potter?*, not only concludes that "it is lawful for them [kids] to read *Harry Potter*" but that the mega-series can be "*profitable* for the body of Christ [the Church]."[2] Two of Neal's chapter titles include: "Use *Harry Potter* to Help Kids Grow in Goodness," and "Using *Harry Potter* to Preach the Gospel." Other pro-*Potter* books written by Christian authors include: *God, the Devil*, and *Harry Potter: A Christian Minister's Defense of the Beloved Novels* (St. Martin's Griffin, 2004) by Presbyterian pastor John Killinger; and *Looking for God in Harry Potter*, by John Granger (Tyndale House Publishing, 2004). Each of these books seeks to discover Jesus Christ within those oft-banished pages.

Author John Granger concludes:

It's a story that resonates with the Great Story for which we are all designed...Harry is a Christian hero parents can joyfully share with their families...J.K. Rowling's books are filled to the brim with Christian themes, imagery, virtues, meaning, implicit and almost explicit, and this is the reason, oddly enough, that the books are so popular. The human heart longs to experience the Christian message, even imaginary experience, and Harry Potter "smuggles the Gospel" better than anyone![3]

Many pro-*Harry* Christians hotly oppose other Christians who don't share their views. Minister Rachel Berry of Good Samaritan United Methodist Church is an example. "Lighten up," she suggests in one interview. "The magic is so tongue-and-cheek."[4] Berry's husband, Pastor John Krapps, affirmed his wife by saying, "We love Harry Potter, and our whole family is outraged by the opposition of the Christian right."[5] Pastor Krapps goes on to say, "There are some distinctly Christian themes in those books, so much so that I'd like to preach a sermon on Harry Potter."[6] Many have. *Potter*-preachers exist also.

Don Compier of the Episcopal Church Divinity School of the Pacific (Berkeley, CA) fully agrees with the Krapps' stance, declaring that *Harry Potter* "stands in the tradition of great British fantasy in which biblical themes and metaphors are wrestling around in powerful ways."[7] Compier compares the orphaned wizard-boy's magical abilities to the "divine gift bestowed by the Holy Spirit at Pentecost,"[8] and even compares Harry to biblical prophets, stating, "The prophets bring down rain and stars from heaven. So I am incredulous that people find Harry Potter to be satanic. There's a long-standing Christian tradition that there are powers in the world—powers for good and evil. And in the end, as happens in *Harry Potter*, the good wins out."[9]

On the opposite side is ex-Wiccan Alison Lentini, a frequent contributor to the highly acclaimed *Spiritual Counterfeits Projects Journal*. In a widely read article entitled, *Harry Potter: Occult Cosmology and the Corrupted Imagination*, Lentini strongly disagreed with Neal, Killinger, Granger, Krapps, Compier, and anyone else supporting their views, countering:

> Harry Potter, an alienated foster child who finds a surrogate family among his peers at Hogwarts, is an apt hero for a generation whose spiritual development has largely been sacrificed to the societal gods of materialism and individualism.[10]

THE CONTROVERSY: Is Harry Healthy for Kids?

In the rush to embrace Harry as a hero capable of inducing a mass surrender of television remote controls and a return to the written word, one of the first casualties was the abandonment of a biblically informed caution about things magical.[11]

For those who seek conformity with the teachings of the Hebrew Scriptures and the New Testament, "safe magic" is wishful thinking, intellectual dishonesty, and an invitation to spiritual deviations that the Hebrew prophets bluntly referred to as "harlotry," and the New Testament apostles forbade. As such, the "safe magic" of Harry Potter offers a message that is as morally confusing to a generation of children as the current ideology of "safe sex."[12]

Berit Kjos, in "Bewitched by Harry Potter," agrees with Lentini:

These stories are every bit as spiritual as Christian literature, but the spiritual power they promote comes from other gods. If you treasure God's truth, may I suggest you encourage your children not to read these books? I know, such parental intervention sounds grossly offensive, in fact, downright Mugglish, to children who love Harry's magical world and reject biblical absolutes. Yet, just as "progressive" leaders fear the influence of biblical truth on budding world citizens, so Christian parents need to guard their children against all kinds of occult "counsel."

Shun other gods. It's tempting to believe the beckoning voices that display enticing counterfeits of all God's wonderful promises. *The power is within yourself*, they say.

Don't listen to the lies.[13]

Ex-occultist Stephen Dollins, in *Under the Spell of Harry Potter* (The Prophecy Club, 2001), is even bolder by associating Pottermania with the direct work of the devil, declaring:

So, here is Satan's plan: You whet the appetites of children who are confused and not quite grounded in family morals, values, and standards (especially those young enough [and] not fully grounded in their faith in Jesus) and introduce them to Harry Potter, a boy wizard who learns and practices the art of Witchcraft and Sorcery. You then bolster their interest in these practices and instill in them the idea that there is no good or evil, only magic, and that it's okay to practice Witchcraft, because it is a moral, wholesome thing to do, as well as the fact that you will receive a reward from it. Finally, when their interest in these practices is at its highest peak, offer the use of the Internet, which is exploding with information that is theirs for the taking, and teaches them how they too **can be just like Harry Potter!** From what the Lord has shown me thus far, I believe this is the strategy Satan is using to recruit our children into his ranks! Our enemy is very cunning, clever, and extremely sneaky. He comes through the "back door" so to speak, rather than coming at us with a "frontal" assault, as this would definitely give his plans away.[14]

Confused? You're not the only one. To summarize, in secular society we find mostly Potter supporters, while within Christianity, we see both supporters and critics. And, as you can see from statements like the one from Stephen Dollins, some of the critics are adamant that the entire *Harry Potter* series is really part of a masterfully orchestrated satanic plot to bypass the sleepy spiritual defenses of lazy Christians in order to invade the unsuspecting minds of our kids. Words fly, lines are drawn, emotions sizzle, and the debate rolls on. And don't miss this point: The issue is now not only whether the *Potter* books and films themselves are good or bad, but whether those who support or condemn them are right or wrong. As much as our modern society favors a relative approach, conclusions and value judgments must be made. *Nobody remains neutral about Potter.*

Which side is right? Is *Harry Potter* healthy or harmful, wholesome or poisonous? Those who love Harry often conclude that the Anti-*Potter* Resistance Movement is composed of uninformed, overly scrupulous, narrow-minded souls exhibiting ridiculous paranoia—sort of like the Dursley clan. On the other side, the Just-Say-No-to-*Harry* group often categorizes *Potter* supporters as undiscerning at best, or dreadfully duped by a subtle devil at worst. That's the debate, and whether we like it or not, it's not going away anytime soon.

As you've probably guessed by now, I'm not exactly a *Harry Potter* fan, and throughout the remainder of this controversial book I'll explain my reasons for detecting—borrowing from Richard Abanes—a "menace behind the magic."

Again, some of the main pro-*Potter* arguments are:

1. *Harry Potter* is great because kids are reading instead of watching TV.

2. *Harry Potter* is entirely fictitious, therefore not worth worrying about.

3. *Harry Potter* teaches valuable moral lessons, especially about the universal struggle of good against evil.

Keep reading. It's time to explore the validity of these arguments.

ENDNOTES

1. *TIME Magazine*, June 23, 2003, p. 63.

2. Connie Neal, *What's a Christian to Do With Harry Potter?* (Colorado Springs, CO: Waterbrook Press, 2001), p. 201.

3. Referenced at www.americandaily.com/article/4593.

4. Abanes, *Harry Potter and the Bible*, p. 87.

5. *Ibid.*

6. *Ibid.*

7. *Ibid.*

8. *Ibid.*

9. *Ibid.*

10. *Spiritual Counterfeits Projects (SCP) Journal*, Vol. 23:4-24:1, 2000. *Witchcraft: Spellbinding a Culture*. Article entitled, "Harry Potter: Occult Cosmology and the Corrupted Imagination," by Alison Lentini, p. 34.

11. *Ibid.*, p. 22.

12. *Ibid.*, pp. 24-25.

13. Quoted by Neal in *What's a Christian to Do With Harry Potter?*, pp. 16-17. Source: Berit Kjos, "Bewitched by Harry Potter," Kjos Ministries (December 24, 1999). Available at http://www.crossroad.to.

14. Stephen Dollins, *Under the Spell of Harry Potter*, Stephen Dollins and *The Prophecy Club* (2001), pp. 95-96.

CHAPTER 5

THE CHARM:
Johnny Is Reading a Book!

*The stories of childhood leave an indelible impression,
and their author always has a niche in the temple of memory.*
—Howard Pyle (1853-1911); Writer, Illustrator

The *Harry*-gets-kids-to-read argument is the one I hear most. Because TV-saturated boys and girls are switching off the tube to absorb 700-page books, *Harry Potter* seems incontrovertibly positive to countless parents. "Johnny's reading a book!" mom says with a smile.

Let's think this through a bit. There's no question that reading a book *can* be good, but is the mere act of reading inherently virtuous? Obviously, if 14-year-old Johnny found a copy of *Playboy* or *Hustler* magazine one afternoon and skipped Nintendo to read erotic articles and look at girly photos, few parents would be thrilled. True, this is an extreme example, but it still illustrates the principle that *what* one reads is more important than simply positioning one's face over a page of words.

Richard Abanes comments:

Parents have accepted the highly flawed and perilous idea that *any* reading is better than *no* reading. Many parents now believe that reading is intrinsically good regardless of the quality of the material being read.[1]

Abanes is correct. Such reasoning *is* "highly flawed and perilous," and really reflects the sad, confused state of modern parenting itself. Too many parents have neglected their God-given responsibility to raise their children to read and love books—wholesome books—and to teach them better ways to utilize their time than spending countless hours viewing *Spiderman* or *Terminator*. The real problem is that so many moms and dads don't have time for their kids, so they plop them before 60-inch, hi-definition, fast-action baby-sitters, letting them watch whatever Hollywood rolls out. Then when some mesmerizing novel like *Harry Potter* grips Johnny's chronically short attention span so that he finally pokes the "power off" button, mom's ecstatic.

"Look honey," she reports to her overworked spouse, "Johnny's not watching TV tonight; he's reading a book!" "Cool!" replies the boy's largely absent father. "How's our supply of Starbucks?" Honestly, why haven't these parents taught Johnny to do useful things with himself in the first place? Why are they so thrilled that *Harry Potter* has diverted their son from television? *Isn't there something wrong with this picture?*

Speaking of his 1970s generation, child education expert James E. Higgins declared, "No one has to remind parents that a bad book can seduce."[2] "No one," that is, in the 1970s. Today parents need reminding. "We hold these truths to be self-evident," penned Thomas Jefferson in his immortal Declaration of Independence. It should also be "self-evident" that the mere act of reading is not half as important as what's being read. Why can't everyone see this? It's as plain as the Rabbi being Jewish.

The truth is: Books are a powerful force for good or evil, for they reflect the minds, beliefs, convictions, and characters of their authors. Books can inspire honesty, integrity, purity, self-control, nobility, and adherence to right principles, or they can seductively draw our inherently fallen nature toward dishonesty, impurity, self-centeredness, rebellion, and sin. There's a mysterious spirituality—both good and bad—working through books, music, and television. These all influence thought, shape ideas, mold character, motivate action, affect society, and yes, even impact human destiny.

Alison Lentini, in her article entitled, "Harry Potter: Occult Cosmology and the Corrupted Imagination," forcefully reminds us of the impact of even fiction stories:

> The stories that we choose, both as individuals and societies, define our subsequent histories...Stories do indeed matter, functioning as cornerstones, windows, and roadmaps.[3]

Stories, newspapers, magazines, and books pack powerful punches. "The American press is the most powerful force on the planet," says Leann Phenix, founder of Phenix and Phenix Literary Publicists, Inc. The motto of her company is: "We believe books change lives..." It's the truth. Famed essayist Henry David Thoreau (1817-1862) understood this principle fully, commenting: "How many a man has dated a new era in his life from reading a book!"

Clearly, books impact not only our natural lives, but also our spiritual lives. Maybe that's why E.N. Kirk penned these memorable words:

> It has not been the devil's policy to keep the masses of mankind in ignorance; but finding that they will read, he is doing all in his power to poison their books.[4]

British historian G.M. Trevelyan (1876-1962) wisely declared that even schools can become corrupt, leading to a generation of students that, while capable of reading, writing, and arithmetic, often fails to discern the difference between wholesome fare and detrimental fluff. "Education," Trevelyan wrote, "has produced a vast population able to read but unable to distinguish what is worth reading, an easy prey to sensations and cheap appeals."[5] As a consequence, John Morely insightfully reflects, "Some of the most famous books are the least worth reading."[6]

It's time to shift gears from mere human productions to Planet Earth's all-time best-selling book, the Holy Bible. By far, it is the most important volume "worth reading." In one of his many New Testament letters, Paul wrote to young Timothy:

> *But you must continue in the things which you have learned and been assured of, knowing from whom you have learned them, and that **from childhood you have known the Holy Scriptures**, which are able to make you wise for salvation through faith which is in Christ Jesus. **All Scripture is given by inspiration of God**, and is profitable for doctrine, for reproof, for correction, for instruction in righteousness, that the man of God may be complete, thoroughly equipped for every good work* (2 Timothy 3:14-17).

Paul affirmed that the "Holy Scriptures" (the Bible) should not only be "learned... from childhood," but that its heavenly, supernatural current can make human beings "wise for salvation." The Bible imparts "instruction in righteousness" and can mold any honest-hearted young person into a noble "man [or woman] of God...thoroughly equipped for every good work." *Such is the power of God's Book*.

The prophet Isaiah urged us to "search from the book of the Lord, and read: Not one of these shall fail" (Isa. 34:16). If today's youth would "search from the book of the Lord, and read"—earnestly, faithfully, and with receptive hearts—many more would have strong, well-balanced, symmetrical characters. There would be less teen drug use, teen alcoholism, teen abortion, teen murder, teen suicide, and all-too-common teenage aimlessness.

In America's early days, the Bible was more highly esteemed by our population generally, and by our country's leadership particularly. Men in high political office—including presidents—weren't ashamed to endorse God's Word publicly. Note these classic remarks from some of America's greatest leaders:

> ABRAHAM LINCOLN (1809-1865): "I believe the Bible is the best gift God has ever given to man."[7]

> DANIEL WEBSTER (1782-1852): "If we abide by the principles taught in the Bible, our country will go on prospering."[8]

JOHN QUINCY ADAMS (1876-1848): "I have made it a practice for several years to read the Bible through in the course of every year."[9]

HORACE GREELEY (1811-1872): "It is impossible to mentally or socially enslave a Bible-reading people."[10]

ROBERT E. LEE (1807-1870): "In all my perplexities and distresses, the Bible has never failed to give me light and strength."[11]

THEODORE ROOSEVELT (1858-1919): "A thorough knowledge of the Bible is worth more than a college education."[12]

GEORGE WASHINGTON (1732-1799): "The perpetuity of this nation depends upon the religious education of the young."[13]

George Washington was America's first president. He wisely understood that the future of our country was dependent upon "the religious education of the young." In older days, such education came from parents and teachers who understood the principle that what Johnny reads is infinitely more important than the mere act of reading itself. Where have such parents gone?

Too often the answer is: To soap operas.

ENDNOTES

1. Richard Abanes, *Fantasy and Your Family: A Closer Look at the Lord of the Rings, Harry Potter, and Magick in the Modern World* (Camp Hill, PA: Christian Publications, Inc. , 2002), p. 41.

2. *Ibid*, p. 45.

3. *SCP Journal*, 23:4-24:1, p. 28.

4. See http://www.nonstopenglish.com/reading/quotations/index.asp?author=E.N.+Kirk.

5. See http://www.cyber-nation.com/victory/quotations/authors/quotes_trevelyan_gm.html.

6. See http://www.yourquotations.net/John%20Morely_quotes.html.

7. Quoted in "Famous People Believed," see http://www.eternalaffairs.com/famouspeoplebelieved.html.

8. *Ibid.*

9. See http://poweredbychrist.homestead.com/radicals.html.

10. See http://www.biblenet.net/library/discover/part1b.html.

11. Quoted in "Famous People Believed," see http://www.eternalaffairs.com/famouspeoplebelieved.html.

12. *Ibid.*

13. Quoted on http://poweredbychrist.homestead.com/radicals.html.

CHAPTER 6

THE SPELL:

It Is Only Fiction!

Fiction is like a spider's web,
attached ever so lightly perhaps,
but still attached to life at all four corners.
Often the attachment is scarcely perceptible.
—Virginia Woolf (1882-1941); British Novelist, Essayist

How about the *Potter*'s-only-fiction argument? Is it valid? First of all, just because a book is fiction, does this mean it has *no effect* on its readers? The sober reality is: *Fiction is a powerful communicator of ideas that influence thought and behavior.* A little familiarity with *Harry Potter* reveals that Mrs. Rowling herself is clearly using the vehicle of fiction as a teaching device to influence the actions of young readers.

At the end of each *Harry Potter* book, Headmaster Albus Dumbledore reflects on the events of the school year and then offers counsel and suggestions to Harry and his fellow Hogwarts students. Some of Dumbledore's suggestions are moral and insightful—which contributes to the argument that these books are good for kids. As I share some of Dumbledore's words, my point here is simply to show that while Joanne Rowling's books may be classified as fiction, they were definitely written not only to entertain, but to teach. Once this is proven, in later chapters, we'll go beyond these apparently "good" lessons to see what other ideas are entering youthful, receptive minds.

Near the end of the very first book, *Harry Potter and the Sorcerer's Stone*, Mrs. Rowling concludes with Albus Dumbledore making this comment to young Harry:

> "The truth," Dumbledore sighed, "It is a very beautiful and terrible thing, and should therefore be treated with great caution."[1]

Here Rowling is clearly using the vehicle of fiction to teach her readers about the nature of "truth." In essence, what Professor Dumbledore said is correct. Truth is beautiful and terrible, should never be taken lightly, and should be handled with great care and respect. The fact that such a lesson comes from a sorcerer who heads up an institution teaching witchcraft to teenagers will be considered more fully later. My point here is simply that Rowling *is using the fictitious character of Albus Dumbledore to teach practical lessons to kids*, and no amount of it's-only-fiction reasoning can get around this "truth."

Professor Dumbledore continues by explaining to the astonished young Harry why he was able to escape Professor Quirrell—a Death Eater in disguise—and Lord Voldemort's deadly grasp:

> "Your mother died to save you. If there is one thing Voldemort cannot understand, it is love. He didn't realize that love as powerful as your mother's for you leaves its own mark. Not a scar, no visible sign...to have been loved so deeply, even though the person who loved us is gone, will give us some protection forever. It is in your very skin. Quirrell, full of hatred, greed, and ambition, sharing his soul with Voldemort, could not touch you for this reason. It was agony to touch a person marked by something so good."[2]

Here Albus Dumbledore comments about Harry Potter's mother who died to save him, about love itself, and about its deeply sacrificial nature in contrast to hatred, greed, and ambition. Again, there's much truth here; and taken by themselves, these words not only teach a lesson—*but a deeply spiritual one.* It's hard to imagine Mrs. Rowling writing this without wanting to influence her young reader's actions. Of course, we all want our children to have loving and unselfish hearts—but is the occult an appropriate teaching context? Think for a moment: If kids can absorb lessons from Headmaster Dumbledore about love and being "marked by something so good," isn't it reasonable to assume they can also be influenced by other lessons in the very same books that aren't so good? To deny this possibility is naïve.

Two pages away from his "good" lesson, Dumbledore tells Harry about his dead friend, Nicolas Flamel, and Nicolas' wife, Perenelle. Surprisingly, both Nicolas Flamel and Perenelle really existed (more on this later). Rowling writes:

> Dumbledore smiled at the look of amazement on Harry's face. "To one as young as you, I'm sure it seems incredible, but to Nicolas and Perenelle, it is really like going to bed after a very, *very* long day. After all, to the well-organized mind, death is but the next great adventure."[3]

Thus, two pages away from Dumbledore's lesson about treating truth cautiously and the importance of sacrificial love, the Headmaster of Hogwarts School of Witchcraft and Wizardry comments about a real historical personage, Nicolas Flamel, and about the nature of death itself. Dumbledore said Flamel had a "well-organized mind" which understood that "death is but the next great adventure." *Is this the truth?* In Chapter 10 of this book we'll discover what the Bible says about what happens to sorcerers after death. Stay with me...

Joanne Rowling's second book is *Harry Potter and the Chamber of Secrets.* Characteristically, near its conclusion Professor Dumbledore again teaches a lesson about why the Sorting Hat—a magical hat that decides which dormitory students will stay in—yielded to Harry Potter's wishes by putting him in the "good" dorm (Gryffindor) instead of Slytherin, which was the dorm that Tom Riddle (who became Voldemort) stayed in, and out of which most Dark Wizards come:

"It only put me in Gryffindor," said Harry in a defeated voice, "because I asked not to go in Slytherin"... "*Exactly*," said Dumbledore, beaming once more. "Which makes you *very different* from Tom Riddle. It is our choices, Harry, that show what we truly are, far more than our abilities."[4]

Here Dumbledore stresses the importance of our choices affecting our futures, even beyond our circumstances and abilities. This is true, and once again, Mrs. Rowling is clearly not just a writer of fiction, but a *teacher of young readers*. Yet taken in context, Harry Potter's good decision was to choose the Gryffindor dorm above the Slytherin dorm inside a sorcery school. In our real world, would this be a wise choice? Only if witchcraft is a science that can be practiced wisely. Is it? We'll find out in Chapter 10.

Near the end of book three, *Harry Potter and the Prisoner of Azkaban*, Harry's actions resulted in the merciful sparing of the life of Peter Pettigrew, a servant of Voldemort, who escaped to rejoin his master. Dumbledore comments to Harry:

"Pettigrew owes his life to you. You have sent Voldemort a deputy who is in your debt...When one wizard saves another wizard's life, it creates a certain bond between them...and I'm much mistaken if Voldemort wants his servant in the debt of Harry Potter."

"I don't want a connection with Pettigrew!" said Harry. "He betrayed my parents!"[5]

Dumbledore replies:

"This is magic at its deepest, its most impenetrable, Harry. But trust me...the time may come when you will be very glad you saved Pettigrew's life."[6]

Here, the man who teaches Harry Potter practical lessons about truth, greed, hatred, death, choices, and sacrificial love, now calls the results of Harry's actions "magic at its deepest, its most impenetrable."

Lesson learned? *Witchcraft's magic has deep and benevolent qualities worth contemplating.*

Book four is called *Harry Potter and the Goblet of Fire*. Near the end, Harry sneaks into Dumbledore's private office to make use of one of his occult tools. He's caught, and should be reprimanded, yet Dumbledore justifies Harry's inappropriate actions, declaring:

> "I was using the Pensieve... and put it away rather hastily. Undoubtedly I did not fasten the cabinet door properly. Naturally, it would have attracted your attention."

> "I'm sorry," Harry mumbled. Dumbledore shook his head. "Curiosity is not a sin," he said. "But we must exercise caution with our curiosity...yes, indeed..."[7]

Now Dumbledore teaches a lesson about curiosity and sin to his young wizard student—and to all kids reading that *Harry Potter* book. Like truth, love, and death, "sin" is a highly spiritual word, and again, Dumbledore's statement is true, when taken alone. Curiosity isn't a sin, but must be tamed. Yet the context of Albus' statement shows him defending Harry's curiosity about a mysterious Pensieve (a tool for performing magic), even to the extent of justifying the boy's actions of sneaking into his private office and breaking into his cabinet. In real life, one of the biggest issues in the raging *Potter* controversy concerns whether or not Rowling's books might cause some young readers to develop a curiosity about the occult. In the above instance, the context of Dumbledore's message to Harry doesn't discourage such interest. Instead, he counsels caution. In a later chapter of this book, we'll look more carefully at what the Bible says about sin, including "the sin of witchcraft" (1 Sam. 15:23), and about the dangers inherent in becoming curious *about it*.

The last section we'll explore in this chapter comes at the conclusion of the same book, *Harry Potter and the Goblet of Fire*. In his usual end-of-the-year speech before the entire student body of young sorcerers attending Hogwarts, Headmaster Dumbledore remarks:

"The end," said Dumbledore, looking around at them all, "of another year."

He paused, and his eyes fell upon the Hufflepuff table. Theirs had been the most subdued table before he had gotten to his feet, and theirs were still the saddest and palest faces in the Hall.

"There is much that I would like to say to you all tonight," said Dumbledore, "but I must first acknowledge the loss of a very fine person, who should be sitting here," he gestured toward the Hufflepuffs, "enjoying our feast with us. I would like for you all, please, to stand, and raise your glasses to Cedric Diggory."

They did it, all of them; the benches scraped as everyone in the Hall stood, and raised their goblets, and echoed, in one loud, low, rumbling voice, "Cedric Diggory"...

"Cedric was a person who exemplified many of the qualities that distinguish Hufflepuff House," Dumbledore continued. "He was a good and loyal friend, a hard worker, who valued fair play. His death has affected you all, whether you knew him or not. I think that you have the right, therefore, to know exactly how it came about."

Harry raised his head and stared at Dumbledore.

"Cedric Diggory was murdered by Lord Voldemort."

A panicked whisper swept the Great Hall. People were staring at Dumbledore in disbelief, in horror. He looked perfectly calm as he watched them mutter themselves into silence. "The Ministry of Magic," Dumbledore continued, "does not wish me to tell you this. It is possible that some of your parents will be horrified that I have done so—either because they will not believe that Lord Voldemort has returned, or because they think I should not tell you, as young as you are. It is my belief, however, that truth is generally preferable to lies, and that any attempt to pretend that Cedric died as a result of an accident, or some sort of blunder of his own, is an insult to his memory....

"There is somebody else who must be mentioned in connection with Cedric's death," Dumbledore went on. "I am talking, of course, about Harry Potter."

A kind of ripple crossed the Great Hall as a few heads turned in Harry's direction before flicking back to the face of Dumbledore.

"Harry Potter managed to escape Lord Voldemort," said Dumbledore. "He risked his own life to return Cedric's body to Hogwarts. He showed, in every respect, the sort of bravery that few wizards have ever shown in facing Lord Voldemort, and for this, I honor him."

Dumbledore turned gravely to Harry and raised his goblet once more. Nearly everyone in the Great Hall followed suit...

When everyone had once again resumed their seats, Dumbledore continued, "The Triwizard Tournament's aim was to further and promote magical understanding. In the light of what has happened—of Lord Voldemort's return—such ties are more important than ever before."

Dumbledore looked from Madame Maxime and Hagrid, to Fleur Delacour and his fellow Beauxbatons students, to Viktor Krum and the Durmstrangs at the Slytherin table...

"Every guest in this Hall," said Dumbledore, and his eyes lingered upon the Durmstrang students, "will be welcomed back here any time, should they wish to come. I say to you all, once again—in the light of Voldemort's return, we are only as strong as we are united, as weak as we are divided. Lord Voldemort's gift for spreading discord and enmity is very great. We can fight it only by showing an equally strong bond of friendship and trust. Differences of habit and language are nothing at all if our aims are identical and our hearts are open.

"It is my belief—and never have I so hoped that I am mistaken—that we are all facing dark and difficult times. Some of you in this Hall have already suffered directly at the hands of Lord Voldemort. Many of your families have been torn asunder. A week ago, a student was taken from our midst. Remember Cedric. Remember, if the time should come when you have to make a choice between what is right and what is easy, remember what happened to a boy who was good, and kind, and brave, because he strayed across the path of Lord Voldemort. Remember Cedric Diggory."[8]

An objective analysis of this section should leave no doubt in any candid mind that Joanne Kathleen Rowling is definitely attempting *to teach* certain values and ideas to young people. There's no question about it. There's also no question that many of the words within Dumbledore's speech, taken by themselves, are true, valid, and insightful. The Headmaster emphasizes the importance of truth above lies, extols bravery, and sets forth the virtuous qualities of a dead boy who "was a good and loyal friend, a hard worker, who valued fair play." The Head Sorcerer also urged his students to choose "what is right" above "what is easy"—a lesson much-needed today.

By now you should be able to discern something of Potter Power and why millions are convinced that these novels should be incorporated into the United States public school system. The idea is: They're great teaching tools to instill values into mixed-up young people. Yet once again this very argument proves that people recognize that the *Harry Potter* books *do teach things to kids*. I agree. They surely do. I also agree that being a loyal friend, a hard worker, practicing fair play, and being good, kind, and brave, are virtues needed by our youth today. (I'm sure Mrs. Rowling wants to teach these good things.)

But wait a minute. Once we are honest enough to admit that the *Harry Potter* books *do* teach values, here's that same sober question we asked before: Is it reasonable to assume that the *only* values kids will learn from those witchcraft-made-funny pages are good ones? I don't think so. The truth is—and you'll see this soon—the *Harry Potter* books teach much more than what appears on the surface, such as *the value of being a good witch* and the importance of occult practitioners sticking together with those who are like-minded.

In that very same speech Dumbledore confessed that "The Triwizard Tournament's *aim was to further and promote magical understanding....*" Could this be one of J.K. Rowling's purposes as well? Of course, I know there's no such thing as a Triwizard Tournament. Yet it's equally true that around the world there are real witches now seeking "to further and promote magical understanding" about Wicca witchcraft—and Dumbledore's words fit nicely with their goals. Dumbledore also encouraged his Hogwarts students not to let any differences, discord, or enmity prevent their unity, declaring, "We are only as strong as we are united, as weak as we are divided." Lessons learned: (1) Unity is good, and (2) *Witches should be united.*

Albus Dumbledore says, "Truth is generally preferable to lies." This isn't right. Truth is *always* preferable to lies. Soon we'll look at what the Bible says about truth, lies, wizards, sorcery, and about a brilliant yet fallen angel named lucifer who has become a master of mingling truth with error to accomplish his infernal purposes.

ENDNOTES

1. Rowling, *Sorcerer's Stone*, p. 298.
2. Rowling, *Sorcerer's Stone*, p. 299.
3. Rowling, *Sorcerer's Stone*, p. 297.
4. Rowling, *Chamber of Secrets*, p. 333.
5. Rowling, *Prisoner of Azkaban*, p. 427.
6. *Ibid.*
7. Rowling, *Goblet of Fire*, p. 598.
8. Rowling, *Goblet of Fire*, pp. 721-724.

CHAPTER 7

THE POTION:

Mixing Fantasy With Reality

*You have to learn the subtle science and exact art of
potion-making [to] understand the beauty of the softly sim-
mering cauldron with its shimmering fumes, the
delicate power of liquids that creep through human
veins, bewitching the mind, ensnaring the senses....*
—Professor Snape to Hogwarts students[1]

Those who constantly repeat the *Harry*'s-fiction-thus-harmless
argument often overlook these basic, incontrovertible facts:

1. Fiction is a powerful communicator of ideas that influ-
    ence beliefs, character, and behavior, especially in
    young readers.

2. Mrs. Rowling's books *do* teach values—even spiritual
    ones. Some are good, but others are now causing great
    concern to those who believe what God's Word teaches
    about witchcraft and sorcery.

3. The entire *Harry Potter* series is permeated with refer-
    ences to real-life, non-fiction places, persons, and com-
    mon occult practices that make it vastly different from

other productions usually classified as "Children's Fantasy Literature."

I call point number three, *The Potion: Mixing Fantasy with Reality.* Let's turn our attention to this subtle brew.

First of all, it's obvious to those who have actually sat down and read the *Harry Potter* novels that they're filled with entirely fictitious things most kids know aren't real, such as fire-breathing dragons, a high-flying wizard sport called Quidditch, a wizard jail named Azkaban, slimy creatures called dementors that suck out their victims' souls, spells that turn humans into toads, quirky house elves, and even a wizard bank run by goblins. J.K. Rowling has quite an imagination, and it's primarily because of these *obviously unreal elements* that most parents and teachers dismiss the books as simply "good ol' fashioned fun."

Yet there's a flip side to this coin. *Harry Potter* is also jam-packed with references to real-life places, persons, and practices, many of which are surprising. To begin with, here's one unusual example. In *Harry Potter and the Order of the Phoenix*, a man named Arthur Weasley is viciously attacked by Voldemort and rushed, half-dead, to a wizard hospital called St. Mungos. Harry Potter and Weasley relatives hasten to visit the wounded man. At the nurse's station, the Weasley party inquires into Arthur's whereabouts:

> "Arthur Weasley?" said the witch, running her finger down a long list in front of her.

> "Yes, first floor, second door on the right. Dai Llewellyn ward."[2]

Dai Llewellyn ward? Believe it or not, *Llewellyn* is the name of one of the largest publishers of occult literature in our modern world! Llewellyn Publications, in St. Paul, Minnesota, publishes *Silver Ravenwolf's, Teen Witch: Wicca for a New Generation*, and hundreds of other occult titles. Not only that, but Llewellyn Publications also has a real-life, spell-filled, witchcraft-saturated web site dedicated exclusively to teenagers![3] Whether Rowling chose "Llewellyn" as a code word for insiders who know the terms, or whether its usage simply reveals her familiarity with real occultism—I can't say. But I know this: Its usage subtly connects *Harry Potter and the Order of the Phoenix* with real witchcraft and is typical of her potion—mixing fantasy with reality.

The very beginning of the first book, *Harry Potter and the Sorcerer's Stone*, opens with the Dursley family living in England, and then refers to real places like Kent, Yorkshire, Surrey, the Isle of Wight, and the famous King's Cross subway station in London, from which Harry catches a train to Hogwarts. The Dursleys are also portrayed as real people who fight traffic jams, watch the nightly news on TV, own computers and VCRs, and are incorrigibly prejudiced against anyone who practices magic (more on this later).

The *Harry Potter* books also mention Brazil, Egypt, France, Albania, Australia, Ireland, Peru, Bulgaria, England, Wales, Uganda, Scotland, Luxembourg, and Norway.[4] At one international wizard event Harry attended:

> Three African wizards sat in serious conversation, all of them wearing long white robes and roasting what looked like a rabbit on a bright purple fire, while a group of middle-aged American witches sat gossiping happily beneath a spangled banner stretched between their tents that read: THE SALEM WITCHES INSTITUTE.[5]

This event is clearly fiction, yet "African wizards" and "American witches" exist today. And, as many kids learn in school, there were real people living in Salem, Massachusetts, who were accused of practicing witchcraft in 1692. Twenty were executed (19 by hanging) during one of the most publicized witch trials in history. To research historical facts, simply visit the web site of the Salem Witch Museum at http://www.salemwitchmuseum.com.

During a typical school year at Hogwarts, students are often allowed to visit a nearby witch-village named Hogsmead, "the only all-wizard village in Britain...."[6] "Hogsmead" doesn't exist, but Britain surely does. Ask Joanne Rowling. She grew up there.

Near the end of *Harry Potter and the Sorcerer's Stone*, Harry asks Dumbledore:

"But your friend—Nicolas Flamel—"

"Oh, you know about Nicolas?" said Dumbledore, sounding quite delighted.[7]

As mentioned previously, Nicolas Flamel was a real person. In fact, he has quite a reputation within historical, occult lore. Researcher Richard Abanes comments:

Nicholas [sic.] Flamel really existed. He was a French alchemist who allegedly succeeded in making the Philosopher's Stone in the late 1300's. According to historical documents and occult tradition, Flamel learned how to make the Philosopher's Stone through the esoteric *Book of Abraham the Jew*. This text, supposedly written by the Jewish Patriarch, contained various directions in hieroglyphic form. Alchemists throughout the centuries have believed that after deciphering the drawings, Flamel did indeed create the Philosopher's Stone, and by so doing, never died.[8]

Near the beginning of *Harry Potter and the Sorcerer's Stone*, in preparation for his first semester at Hogwarts, Harry was given a list of required "Course Books," which included:

The Standard Book of Spells (Grade 1) by Miranda Goshawk
A History of Magic by Bethilda Bagshot
Magical Theory by Aldabert Waffling
One Thousand Magical Herbs and Fungi by Phyllida Spore
Magical Drafts and Potions by Arsenius Jigger[9]

These exact book titles may be fictitious, yet similar titles written by Wiccan authors can be found all over the Net, such as *The Complete Book of Spells, Ceremonies, and Magic*, by Migene Gonzalez-Wippler (1998), *The History of Magic*, by Eliphas Levi (1997), *Encyclopedia of Magical Herbs*, by Scott Cunningham (1985) and *Magick Potions:*

THE POTION: Mixing Fantasy With Reality

How to Prepare and Use Homemade Oils, Aphrodisiacs, Brews, and Much More, by Gurina Dunwich (1998).

How about the authors on Harry's list? Most are fictitious, except Aldabert Waffling. Abanes comments:

> Rowling mixes reality with fantasy in her series...Aldabert [Waffling] was a French pseudo-mystic who claimed he could foretell the future and read thoughts. *The Encyclopedia of Occultism and Parapsychology* reveals that "[H]e was in the habit of giving away parings of his nails and locks of his hair as powerful amulets [charms used to drive away evil]. He is said to have even set up an altar in his own name."...He also invoked demons using mystical prayers he had composed. The Church convicted him of sorcery in 744-745 A.D., and condemned him to perpetual imprisonment in the monastery of Fulda.[10]

Another highly unusual name occurs inside the third *Harry Potter* book. Near the end of another dreadfully boring summer at the Dursleys and in preparation for an action-packed school year at Hogwarts, Harry again visits Diagon Alley inside London, a "long cobbled street packed with the most fascinating wizarding shops in the world."[11] There:

> Harry ate breakfast each morning in the Leaky Cauldron, where he liked watching the other guests: funny little witches from the country, up for a day's shopping; venerable-looking wizards arguing over the latest article in *Transfiguration Today*; wild-looking warlocks; raucous dwarfs; and once, what looked suspiciously like a hag, who ordered a plate of raw liver from behind a thick woolen balaclava.[12]

Entering a bookstore to purchase schoolbooks, Harry told the manager:

> "I need *Unfogging the Future* by Cassandra Vablatsky."...
> "Here you are," said the manager, who had climbed a set of steps to take down a thick, black-bound book. "*Unfogging*

the Future. Very good guide to all your basic fortune-telling methods—palmistry, crystal balls, bird entrails—."[13]

As with "Llewellyn," only informed occultists will catch it. By slightly rearranging "Vabl" in "*Vabl*atsky," you get, "Blavatsky." So what? *Helena Petrovna Blavatsky* (1831-1891) was a real British woman who is now internationally recognized as one of the most influential occult leaders of all time. She "was the founder of Theosophy, an occult blending of metaphysical thought, spiritualism, channeling, science, Eastern philosophy, Transcendental and mental healing," says Abanes.[14] In one of Blavatsky's many articles, she even referred to Aldabert Waffling, calling him "famous...in the annals of magic."[15] We also know that Rowling is no stranger to rearranging letters. She did it in *Harry Potter and the Chamber of Secrets* when Lord Voldemort wrote his original name and then scrambled the words:

> He [Tom Riddle] pulled Harry's wand from his pocket and began to trace it through the air, writing three shimmering words,

> TOM MARVOLO RIDDLE

> Then he waved the wand once, and the letters of his name re-arranged themselves:

> I AM LORD VOLDEMORT[16]

Just like the title, *Harry Potter and the Chamber of Secrets*, it seems Rowling's books have hidden occult secrets as well. Far from being simply an imaginative children's book writer, J.K. Rowling is also a thorough researcher who earned a Masters degree in Mythology from Exeter University in England. This lady has "an extremely well-developed and sophisticated knowledge of the occult world, its legends, history and nuances."[17] When pressed during an interview on *The Diane Rehm Show*, Mrs. Rowling openly admitted that one-third of her *Harry Potter* material is based on actual occultism.[18]

It is not hard to prove either. In addition to *real places* such as Great Britain, Africa, Ireland, Egypt, Australia, and America, *real*

The Potion: Mixing Fantasy With Reality

names such as Nicolas Flamel, Aldabert Waffling, and Helena Blavatsky, *real organizations* such as Llewellyn Publications in Minnesota, and *real tools* such as wands, cauldrons, and crystal balls, there's also plenty of *real occult practices*. Spell-casting, numerology, fortune-telling, divination, astrology, palmistry, charms, crystal gazing, out-of-body travel, and spirit-channeling are all mentioned in Rowling's occult-laden pages. It's true, most of these references are carefully mingled with silly and imaginary elements, yet this sober fact remains: These practices are *real* and are practiced today by *real* witches, Wiccans, and sorcerers all over Planet Earth. For proof, simply visit any Barnes & Noble bookstore and browse through the occult section. Scary isn't it? Especially when we realize kids are devouring these books!

The following quotes, directly from the *Harry Potter* books, not only describe objects and practices with real counterparts in the real world of Wicca witchcraft, but they've been written in such a way so as to make them soothingly appealing, mystically inviting, and super exciting to young people. See for yourself.

Book one, *Harry Potter and the Sorcerer's Stone*, depicts Harry seeking "A magic wand…this was what Harry had been really looking forward to."[19] Wanting the right wand, Harry goes to Diagon Alley in London and visits "Ollivanders: Makers of Fine Wands since 382 B.C."[20] After trying a few magic sticks that didn't feel quite right, Harry grabbed one particular piece of wood and "felt a sudden warmth in his fingers. He raised the wand above his head, brought it swooshing down through the dusty air and a stream of red and gold sparks shot from the end like a firework, throwing dancing spots of light on to the walls."[21]

Sound neat? All a kid has to do is type the word "wand" into the search field of Yahoo, Google, Ask Jeeves, or any other Internet search engine, and he'll find lots of merchants selling real ones. At Hogwarts, Harry was asked by one of his occult professors, "Have you not read what is to come in the movements of the planets?"[22] This is astrology—a real practice in the real world. Needing more instruction, Harry's told to:

"Lie back on the floor," said Firenze in his calm voice, "and observe the heavens. Here is written, for those who can see, the fortune of our races." Firenze pointed to the red star directly above Harry. "In the past decades, the indications have been that Wizard-kind is living through nothing more than a brief calm between two wars. Mars, bringer of battle, shines brightly above us, suggesting that the fight must break out again soon. How soon, centaurs may attempt to divine by the burning of certain herbs and leaves, by the observation of fume and flame…" It was the most unusual lesson Harry had ever attended.[23]

Lesson indeed! Not only was Harry Potter learning about real astrology, but so is *every kid who reads this*. Millions of human beings today really believe that planetary movements and star patterns contain secret messages about their personal lives and future. If you doubt this, simply glance at any Astrology Forecast or Horoscope while strolling past cash registers to purchase avocados or Kellogg's cereal at Wal-Mart, K-Mart, Albertsons, or any grocery store. Why do these stores carry such things? *Because people believe them and buy them.*

Hermione Granger, one of Harry's closest friends, excelled in sorcery studies above her peers. During her first year at Hogwarts:

Hermione rolled up the sleeves of her gown, flicked her wand, and said, "Wingardium Leviosa!" Their feather rose off the desk and hovered about four feet above their heads.

"Oh, well done!" cried Professor Flitwick, clapping. "Everyone see here, Miss Granger's done it!"[24]

Here strong encouragement is given to those mastering the art of witchcraft.

"Meanwhile, hidden from the teachers, a roaring trade in talismans, amulets, and other protective devices was sweeping the school."[25] More real objects again. Talismans and amulets—often used in astrology—can easily be purchased online at any one of countless occult web sites. In real occultism, practitioners advance from level to level, from beginners to experts. *The exact same principle is taught at Hogwarts.* Concerned that Harry might be woefully unprepared for his next encounter with Voldemort, one teacher offered him advanced instruction:

> Professor Lupin had taken out his own wand, and indicated Harry should do the same. "The spell I am going to try and teach you is highly advanced magic, Harry—well beyond Ordinary Wizarding Level. It is called the Patronus Charm."[26]

One mysterious day, Harry climbed a creaky stairway high in the Hogwarts castle to the Tower Room for a private meeting with his Divination teacher. "Professor Trelawney sat waiting for him before a large crystal ball."[27] Crystal balls are real occult objects used by fortune-tellers the world over. After their brief visit, the following frightening event scared Harry out of his wits:

> Harry got up, picked up his bag and turned to go, but then a loud, harsh voice spoke behind him. "IT WILL HAPPEN TONIGHT." Harry wheeled around. Professor Trelawney had gone rigid in her armchair; her eyes were unfocused and her mouth sagging. "S-sorry?" said Harry. But Professor Trelawney didn't seem to hear him. Her eyes started to roll. Harry sat there in panic. She looked as though she was about to have some sort of seizure. He hesitated, thinking of running to the hospital wing—and then Professor Trelawney spoke again, in the same harsh voice, quite unlike her own: "THE DARK LORD LIES ALONE AND FRIENDLESS, ABANDONED BY HIS FOLLOWERS. HIS SERVANT HAS BEEN CHAINED THESE TWELVE YEARS. TONIGHT, BEFORE MIDNIGHT...THE SERVANT WILL BREAK FREE AND SET OUT TO REJOIN HIS MASTER. THE DARK LORD WILL RISE AGAIN WITH HIS SERVANT'S AID, GREATER AND MORE TERRIBLE THAN EVER HE WAS. TONIGHT...BEFORE MIDNIGHT...THE SERVANT WILL SET OUT...TO REJOIN...HIS MASTER." Professor Trelawney's head fell forward onto her

chest. She made a grunting sort of noise. Harry sat there, staring at her. Then, quite suddenly, Professor Trelawney's head snapped up again. "I'm so sorry, dear boy," she said dreamily, "the heat of the day, you know…I drifted off for a moment."[28]

Here Professor Trelawney slipped into a trance and a strange voice hissed through her lips. In real life, this is called "channeling." In the last few years, many famous mediums—Jane Roberts, Edgar Cayce, J.Z. Knight, James Van Praagh, and John Edwards—have submitted their bodies to become channels for eerie communications by not-of-this-world entities. The human vessel loses consciousness while another mind speaks through its vocal cords. It's true, in the *Harry Potter* books, Trelawney isn't exactly depicted as a reliable witch, yet even Albus Dumbledore admitted that what occurred in the Tower Room was not only "a real prediction," but that perhaps he should "offer her a pay raise" because of it![29] Thus the highly dangerous occult practice of channeling unknown spirit entities is portrayed *both accurately and positively*.

The list of parallels between the semi-fantasy world of Harry Potter and the real-life world of ancient and modern occultism is endless. There's no question about it: *J.K. Rowling knows her stuff*. In fact, much of the occult information inside the *Potter* novels is so real that during one call-in radio interview an eager inquirer asked Rowling if she herself was a member of the "Craft." When she replied with an unexpected "No," the caller said, "You've done your homework quite well." This person then expressed his deep love for the *Harry Potter* books because they not only portray his own beliefs positively but were making his daughter more comfortable with his involvement in real witchcraft.[30]

At the beginning of book three, *Harry Potter and the Prisoner of Azkaban*, Harry is found lying on his stomach in bed, blankets drawn over his head like a tent, so he can read *A History of Magic* by flashlight without the Dursleys glimpsing any light under his bedroom door.

The Potion: Mixing Fantasy With Reality

His class assignment from Hogwarts was, "Witch Burning in the Fourteenth Century Was Completely Pointless—discuss." Turning pages in *A History of Magic*, Harry read:

> Non-magic people (commonly known as Muggles) were particularly afraid of magic in medieval times, but not very good at recognizing it. On the rare occasion that they did catch a real witch or wizard, burning had no effect whatsoever. The witch or wizard would perform a basic Flame Freezing Charm and then pretend to shriek with pain while enjoying a gentle, tickling sensation. Indeed, Wendelin the Weird enjoyed being burned so much that she allowed herself to be caught no less than forty-seven times in various disguises.[31]

Here's a perfect example of Rowling's *Potion* in action. Harry read about "medieval times" when people were "particularly afraid of magic." Historically, this is true. Real witch trials and burnings have occurred; especially from 1300 to 1600 (my purpose is not to justify them). Then Mrs. Rowling does something so characteristic of her entire *Harry Potter* series—she trivializes reality by adding imaginary and goofy elements *that fool people into thinking that no serious impressions are being made.* But they are. Peeling away the fiction, what Harry Potter read from *A History of Magic* packs this subtle message for kids: Witches are smart; non-magical folks are stupid (more on this in the next chapter); and any lingering "fear of magic" today is simply a carryover from unenlightened, bygone days—from "medieval times."

Obviously, I can't read Mrs. Rowling's heart, and I don't claim to understand her motives, but after prayerfully reading the first five *Harry Potter* books to know the facts, the overall evidence reveals:

1. Joanne Kathleen Rowling is extremely knowledgeable about the history of real witchcraft and occultism.

2. She has skillfully woven into her *Harry Potter* story line the names of real persons, places, organizations, and practices connected to real sorcery.

3. She apparently favors occult practices in general.

Think about it: Mrs. Rowling is no fool. She obviously knows that society at large remains leery of witchcraft (although this is changing rapidly). So, to protect herself from potential accusation, she's carefully mixed enough humor and fantasy with occult realities so that if anyone cries out, "She's promoting witchcraft!" she and her supporters can easily say, "Oh Hogwarts! Don't be silly. It's just fiction. Can't you see all the imaginary elements?"

Don't be fooled. Discerning eyes will see deeper and will recognize that the *Harry Potter* books *do* teach definite values and that beyond the fantasy, they *do* portray witchcraft positively. These enchanting productions are really like the delicately crafted *Potion* so poignantly described by Professor Snape when he declared eerily:

> "*You have to learn the subtle science* and exact art of potion-making...
>
> [to] understand the beauty of the softly simmering cauldron with its shimmering fumes, the delicate power of liquids that creep through human veins, bewitching the mind, ensnaring the senses..."[32]

J.K. Rowling wrote this. Her words, "You have to learn the subtle science and exact art of potion-making," apply to her own books. Right under the noses of unsuspecting parents, kids *are learning* about the occult through *Harry Potter*. The "delicate power" of a seemingly harmless story that desensitizes young people to the incredible dangers of spirit channeling is "creeping through human veins, bewitching the mind, ensnaring the senses." There's no doubt about it. Despite their "good" lessons, these uniquely written productions with their attractive covers are communicating this definite message to kids of our generation: Witchcraft is cool, and any lingering "fear of magic" is simply an outdated relic of Dark Age foolishness—"medieval ignorance."

The Potion is working.

ENDNOTES

1. Rowling, *Sorcerer's Stone*, pp. 136-137.

2. Rowling, *Order of the Phoenix*, p. 487.

3. See http://teen.llewellyn.com.

4. Rowling, *Goblet of Fire*, pp. 62-64.

5. Rowling, *Goblet of Fire*, p. 82.

6. Rowling, *Goblet of Fire*, p. 319.

7. Rowling, *Sorcerer's Stone*, p. 297.

8. Abanes, *Harry Potter and the Bible*, p. 26; see also Maurice Magree's *Magicians, Seers, and Mystics* (Kessinger Publications, 1997; transl., Reginald Merton), available at www.alchemylab.com.

9. Rowling, *Sorcerer's Stone*, p. 66.

10. Abanes, *Harry Potter and the Bible*, p. 28; Leslie A. Shepard's, *Encyclopedia of Occultism and Parapsychology* (Detroit, MI: Gale Research, 1991), Ch. 1, pp. 6-7.

11. Rowling, *Prisoner of Azkaban*, p. 49.

12. *Ibid.*

13. Rowling, *Prisoner of Azkaban*, p. 53.

14. Abanes, *Harry Potter and the Bible*, p. 28.

15. *Ibid.*, pp. 28-29.

16. Rowling, *Chamber of Secrets*, p. 314.

17. Abanes, *Harry Potter and the Bible*, p. 24.

18. Rowling interview on *The Diane Rehm Show*, WAMU, National Public Radio, October 20, 1999, available at www.wamu.org.

19. Rowling, *Sorcerer's Stone*, p. 81.

20. Rowling, *Sorcerer's Stone*, p. 82.

21. Rowling, *Sorcerer's Stone*, p. 85.

22. Rowling, *Sorcerer's Stone*, p. 257.

23. Rowling, *Order of the Phoenix*, pp. 602-603.

24. Rowling, *Sorcerer's Stone*, p. 171.

25. Rowling, *Chamber of Secrets*, p. 185.

26. Rowling, *Prisoner of Azkaban*, p. 337.

27. Rowling, *Prisoner of Azkaban*, p. 332.

28. Rowling, *Prisoner of Azkaban*, p. 324.

29. Rowling, *Prisoner of Azkaban*, p. 426.

30. WBUR interview of J.K. Rowling, Oct. 12, 1999, available at www.wbur.org. Quoted by Abanes in *Harry Potter and the Bible*, p. 24.

31. Rowling, *Prisoner of Azkaban*, p. 2.

32. Rowling, *Sorcerer's Stone*, pp. 136-137, italics added.

CHAPTER 8

THE MESSAGE:

Magic Versus Muggles

*We acknowledge a depth of power far greater than
the average person...Everyone has these abilities, but
most don't use them, and some people even fear them.
Witches, and other enlightened souls, strive
to strengthen these natural gifts.*

—Silver Ravenwolf in *Teen Witch*
Wicca for a New Generation[1]

still remember the day (during the summer of 2003) when I first decided to read *Harry Potter* to find out for myself what lurked within those best-selling pages. My wife Kristin and I had just moved from
Fort Worth, Texas, to Paso Robles, California, and we were now settled
into our new home. Paso Robles is a quaint, small town, surrounded by
rolling hills and vineyards, with some bookstores. So, I visited
Chelsea's Books to see if *Harry* was there. Of course he was. I bought
the first four novels.

I prayed about this decision, and I prayed again before reading
book one, *Harry Potter and the Sorcerer's Stone*. Some might feel it
wasn't wise to read these books at all. But, as an author doing research
and writing my own book on the topic, I needed to know the facts.

Another consideration was that I often do radio interviews on books I've written. My imagination pictured a caller on a live show demanding, "Have *you* read *Harry Potter?*" If I said, "Nope...sorry," my credibility would vanish. I took the plunge.

Opening the first chapter, I read about the Dursley family living in a small town on the outskirts of London. The drama began like this:

> Mr. and Mrs. Dursley, of number four, Privet Drive, were proud to say that they were perfectly normal, thank you very much. They were the last people you'd expect to be involved in anything strange or mysterious, because they just didn't hold with such nonsense.

> Mr. Dursley was the director of a firm called Grunnings, which made drills. He was a big, beefy man with hardly any neck, although he did have a rather large mustache. Mrs. Dursley was thin and blond and had nearly twice the usual amount of neck, which came in very useful as she spent so much of her time craning over garden fences, spying on neighbors. The Dursleys had a small son called Dudley and in their opinion there was no finer boy anywhere.

> The Dursleys had everything they wanted, but they also had a secret, and their greatest fear was that somebody would discover it. They didn't think they could bear it if anyone found out about the Potters. Mrs. Potter was Mrs. Dursleys' sister, but they hadn't met for several years; in fact, Mrs. Dursley pretended she didn't have a sister, because her sister and her good-for-nothing husband were as unDursleyish as it was possible to be. The Dursleys shuddered to think what the neighbors would say if the Potters arrived in the street. The Dursleys knew that the Potters had a small son, too, but they had never seen him. This boy was another good reason for keeping the Potters away; they didn't want Dudley mixing with a child like that.[2]

A few pages later, Mr. Dursley listens to the nightly news, which reports that strange things are occurring throughout England:

THE MESSAGE: Magic Versus Muggles

Mr. Dursley sat frozen in his armchair. Shooting stars all over Britain? Owls flying by daylight? Mysterious people in cloaks all over the place? And a whisper, a whisper about the Potters....[3]

As the unsuspecting Dursleys tucked in for the night, apparently out of nowhere...

A man appeared on the corner [a] cat had been watching...so suddenly and silently you'd have thought he'd just popped out of the ground. The cat's tail twitched and its eyes narrowed. Nothing like this man had ever been seen on Privet Drive. He was tall, thin, and very old, judging by the silver of his hair and beard, which were both long enough to tuck into his belt. He was wearing long robes, a purple cloak that swept the ground, and high-heeled, buckled boots. His blue eyes were light, bright, and sparkling behind half-moon spectacles... This man's name was Albus Dumbledore.[4]

I kept reading...Harry's parents, James and Lily Potter, had just been murdered by a super-sinister warlock named Lord Voldemort, and Albus Dumbledore, the Headmaster of Hogwarts School of Witchcraft and Wizardry, had come to place the tiny survivor in a little basket on the Dursleys' doorstep. Whispering to another witch accompanying him, Albus explained:

"It's the best place for him," said Dumbledore firmly. "His aunt and uncle will be able to explain everything to him when he's older. I've written them a letter."

"A letter?" repeated Professor McGonagall faintly, sitting back on a wall. "Really, Dumbledore, you think you can explain all this in a letter? These people will never understand him! He'll be famous—a legend—I wouldn't be surprised if today was known as Harry Potter day in the future—there will be books written about Harry—every child in the world will know his name!"

"Exactly," said Dumbledore, looking very seriously over the top of his half-moon glasses. "It would be enough to turn any boy's head. Famous before he can walk and talk! Famous for something he won't even remember! Can't you see how much better off he'll be, growing up away from all that until he's ready to take it?"

Professor McGonagall opened her mouth, changed her mind, swallowed, and then said, "Yes—yes, you're right, of course...."

A breeze ruffled the neat hedges of Privet Drive, which lay silent and tidy under the inky sky, the very last place you would expect astonishing things to happen. Harry Potter rolled over inside his blankets without waking up. One small hand closed on the letter beside him and he slept on, not knowing he was special, not knowing he was famous, not knowing he would be woken in a few hours time by Mrs. Dursley's scream as she opened the front door to put out the milk bottles, nor that he would spend the next few weeks being prodded and pinched by his cousin Dudley...He couldn't have known that at this very moment, people meeting in secret all over the country were holding up their glasses and saying in hushed voices: "To Harry Potter—the boy who lived!"[5]

I closed the book. *What an introduction!* I thought to myself. *If I was an average boy and not a Christian man, after having read this, I would probably want to learn more about the secret world of witches!* Yes indeed.

One sentence was particularly mysterious. Professor McGonagall, a teacher at Hogwarts, mused:

"These people will never understand him! He'll be famous— a legend—I wouldn't be surprised if today was known as Harry Potter day in the future—there will be books written about Harry—every child in the world will know his name!"

This seemed like a prophecy come true. In real life, kids around the world *do* know Harry Potter's name. Thus, a certain element of realism intruded itself, right off the bat, fantasy aside. And the line, "These people will never understand him!" conveyed the idea that those who aren't witches will never grasp the truth.

The Dursleys were people whom wizards sarcastically called "Muggles," that is, those without "a drop of magical blood in their veins."[6] In every *Harry Potter* book, Muggles are mentioned. Muggles are:

...members of the non-magical community...[7]
...non-magic folk...[8]

The world is pictured as:

...the dark Muggle world...[9]

Wizards must only perform magic:

...far from prying Muggle eyes.[10]

There was no mistaking it. Wizards versus Muggles—that was the message.

After Petunia Dursley's unexpected scream, the reluctant family nevertheless took baby Harry in. *Harry Potter and the Sorcerer's Stone* continued:

Dudley looked a lot like Uncle Vernon. He had a large pink face, not much neck, small, watery blue eyes, and thick blond hair that lay smoothly on his thick, fat head. Aunt Petunia often said that Dudley looked like a baby angel—Harry often said that Dudley looked like a pig in a wig.[11]

There are exceptions, but generally speaking, *Harry Potter* books don't flatter Muggles much. Book four injects another round of sarcasm:

By the time Harry arrived in the kitchen, the three Dursleys were already seated around the table. None of them looked up as he entered or sat down. Uncle Vernon's large red face was hidden behind the morning's *Daily Mail*, and Aunt Petunia was cutting a grapefruit into quarters, her lips pursed over her horselike teeth. Dudley looked furious and sulky, and somehow seemed to be taking up even more space than usual. This was saying something, as he always took up an entire side of the square table by himself...Dudley had reached roughly the size and weight of a killer whale.[12]

Harry's childhood with the Dursleys was superbly rotten. While pampered Dudley slept in a normal bedroom, Harry was forced to sleep in a dusty closet beneath the stairs. What a dismal life! Yet everything changed on Harry's 11th birthday. That's when Hagrid, the messenger from Hogwarts, spoke these four life-changing words: "Harry—yer a wizard."[13]

Oh happy day! Harry thought. He was even more surprised "to find out that everyone in the hidden wizarding world knew his name."[14] After packing his bags and purchasing his witchy school supplies in Diagon Alley, Harry hurried toward the King's Cross subway station in London, finally reaching "platform nine and three-quarters, which wasn't visible to the Muggle eye."[15]

Thus Rowling's Magic versus Muggle message is all-pervasive. It permeates every *Harry Potter* book and forms the framework for the entire series. One of Harry's friends, Mrs. Weasley, declares about Muggles: "Bless them, they'll go to any lengths to ignore magic, even if it's staring them in the face."[16] Wizards: 175. Muggles: 0. The score widens at the beginning of book three, *Harry Potter and the Prisoner of Azkaban*:

> The Dursley family of number four, Privet Drive, was the reason that Harry never enjoyed his summer holidays. Uncle Vernon, Aunt Petunia, and their son, Dudley, were Harry's only living relatives. They were Muggles, and they had a very medieval attitude toward magic. Harry's dead parents, who had been a witch and wizard themselves, were never mentioned under the Dursley's roof. For years, Aunt Petunia and Uncle Vernon had hoped that if they kept Harry as downtrodden as

possible, they would be able to squash the magic out of him. To their fury, they had been unsuccessful. These days they lived in terror of anyone finding out that Harry had spent most of the last two years at Hogwarts School of Witchcraft and Wizardry. The most they could do, however, was to lock away Harry's spellbooks, wand, cauldron, and broomstick at the start of the summer break, and forbid him to talk to the neighbors.[17]

As discussed in Chapter 7, "The Potion: Mixing Fantasy With Reality," this paragraph reveals Rowling's typical mingling of facts with fiction. "Muggles" like the Dursleys—young readers are informed—have "a very medieval attitude toward magic," making them superbly unenlightened. The Dursleys even went so far as "to lock away Harry's spellbooks, wand, cauldron, and broomstick." Imagine that! Shame on them! No matter, for despite their ignorant Mugglish maneuvers, they still couldn't "squash the magic out of him." Magic: 275. Muggles: -50.

In *Harry Potter and the Chamber of Secrets*, the ghostly Professor Binns explains to his Hogwarts students while teaching History of Magic:

> "You all know, of course, that Hogwarts was founded over a thousand years ago—the precise date is uncertain—by the four greatest witches and wizards of the age. The four Houses are named after them: Godric Gryffindor, Helga Hufflepuff, Rowena Ravenclaw, and Salazar Slytherin. They built this castle together, far from prying Muggle eyes, for it was an age when magic was feared by common people, and witches and wizards suffered much persecution...Reliable historical sources tell us this much...."[18]

Fantasy mingled with reality again. "Reliable historical sources," said the Hogwarts professor, speak of times "when magic was feared by common people, and witches and wizards suffered much persecution." Historically, this happened, especially in American history—remember the Salem Witch Trials of 1692? Once again, the subtle message to young people is that it's high time for Muggles to wake up and to accept occult magic for what it really is—a great gift to humanity.

The entire *Harry Potter* saga portrays non-magical people as substandard. To be fair, Mrs. Rowling doesn't portray all Muggles as bad. There are some okay ones out there—they just haven't seen the light. It's also true that not all wizards are smart and intelligent. By no means. There are plenty of goofy ones missing some brain cells. Professor Trelawney is a quack, Professor Binns is a ghost, and there are plenty of hags with long noses. But whatever fictitious faults may be seen in certain witches, there's one person whom Rowling consistently portrays as the epitome of wisdom, power, and the deepest magical abilities: Albus Dumbledore.

Consider the following descriptions of Dumbledore, and remember that kids all over Planet Earth are reading them. Before actually meeting Albus himself, Harry Potter picked up a wizard trading card and read:

> ALBUS DUMBLEDORE, CURRENTLY HEADMASTER OF HOGWARTS. Considered by many the greatest wizard of modern times, Dumbledore is particularly famous for his defeat of the dark wizard Grindewald in 1945...and [for] his work on alchemy with his partner, Nicolas Flamel. Professor Dumbledore enjoys chamber music and tenpin bowling.[19]

More fantasy mixed with reality. As we've seen, Nicolas Flamel was a real historical figure—a French alchemist—who lived in the 1300s. "Enjoys chamber music" gives Dumbledore a touch of style, multiplying his admirable qualities. A house elf told Harry:

> "Albus Dumbledore is the greatest headmaster Hogwarts has ever had...[his] powers rival those of He-Who-Must-Not-Be-Named at the height of his strength."[20]

Seen late one night in his office:

> Dumbledore was sitting in a high-backed chair behind his desk; he leaned forward into the pool of candlelight illuminating

the papers laid out before him. He was wearing a magnificently embroidered purple-and-gold dressing gown over a snowy-white night shirt, but seemed wide awake, his penetrating light-blue eyes fixed intently upon Professor McGonagall.[21]

...his long silver beard and half-moon glasses shining brightly in the candlelight.[22]

Defending a student under attack by an out-of-control teacher:

A split second later Dumbledore was on his feet, his wand raised.[23]

Near the end of *Harry Potter and the Goblet of Fire*, a man who had secretly served Lord Voldemort during a school year at Hogwarts attacked Harry Potter. At the height of their death-struggle, just in the nick of time, Dumbledore crashed into the office for the rescue:

"You're mad," Harry said—he couldn't stop himself— "you're mad!" "Mad, am I?" said Moody, his voice rising uncontrollably. "We'll see! We'll see who's mad, now that the Dark Lord has returned, with me at his side! He is back, Harry Potter, you did not conquer him—and now—I conquer you!" Moody raised his wand, he opened his mouth; Harry plunged his own hand into his robes—"*Stupify!*" There was a blinding flash of red light, and with a great splintering and crashing, the door of Moody's office was blasted apart— Moody was thrown backward onto the office floor. Harry, still staring at the place where Moody's face had been, saw Albus Dumbledore, Professor Snape, and Professor McGonagall looking back out of the Foe-Glass. He looked around and saw the three of them standing in the doorway, Dumbledore in front, his wand outstretched. At that moment, Harry fully understood for the first time why people said Dumbledore was the only wizard Voldemort had ever feared. The look on Dumbledore's face as he stared down at the unconscious form of Mad-Eye Moody was more terrible than Harry could have ever imagined. There was no benign smile

81

upon Dumbledore's face, no twinkle in the eyes behind the spectacles. There was cold fury in every line of the ancient face; a sense of power radiated from Dumbledore as though he was giving off burning heat.[24]

Albus Dumbledore, the Headmaster of Hogwarts, one of the "greatest wizards of all time," the hero of Rowling's series next to Harry Potter himself, is seen as in full control, fearfully powerful, a man who radiates such strength "as though he is giving off burning heat." In this scene Dumbledore is endued with almost Messianic qualities. His appearance and facial expression seem like Almighty God on Judgment Day.

Thus the *Harry Potter* books portray the Dursleys in particular and Muggles in general as largely ignorant, while the Master Sorcerer, Albus Dumbledore, is revealed as essentially all-powerful. Quite a positive message on behalf of witchcraft, wouldn't you say? (I'm hoping by now you won't say, "But it's just fiction!") Concerning Rowling's Magic versus Muggle message within *Harry Potter*, Robert Frisken of Christian Community Schools in Australia comments:

> The ordinary person is typified as being bad because they have no (magic) powers, and heroes are the people who are using the occult. [This] is an inversion of morality....[25]

It's the truth. When it comes to the occult, the *Harry Potter* books take generally accepted standards of right and wrong and turn them upside down. Witches are in; Muggles are out. Witches: 1000. Muggles: -500.

To conclude this chapter, there's one more magnetic element within the *Potter* books that can easily pull the heartstrings of young people (and adults as well) toward real witchcraft. Here it is: Those best-selling pages often portray the thrilling world of occult magic (in contrast to Muggleness) *as the one to which Harry really belongs.*

In the beginning of *Harry Potter and the Chamber of Secrets*, Harry is at the Dursleys near the end of another boring summer. Unexpectedly, he's visited in his under-the-stairs bedroom by Dobby the elf who warns him *against* returning to Hogwarts:

> "W-what?" Harry stammered. "But I've got to go back— term starts on September first. It's all that's keeping me going. You don't know what it's like here. I don't belong here. *I belong in your world—at Hogwarts*."[26]

At the start of *Harry Potter and the Order of the Phoenix*, near the end of still another wretched summer, Harry hears something strange:

> Perhaps it hadn't been a magical sound after all. Perhaps he was so desperate for the tiniest sign of contact from *the world to which he belonged* that he was simply overreacting to perfectly ordinary noises.[27]

Slipping out for a night stroll near Privet Drive, suddenly both Harry and his cousin Dudley are viciously attacked by dementors:

> The arrival of the dementors in Little Whinging seemed to have caused a breach in the great, invisible wall that divided the relentlessly non-magical world of Privet Drive and the world beyond.[28]

Harry used magic and rescued them both, but because it's illegal (according to wizard-laws) for an underage wizard to cast spells in front of Muggles, Harry gets into trouble and is called to a hearing before a wizard court of the Ministry of Magic (an international wizard organization monitoring wizard activities). Harry thinks to himself:

> What if they ruled against him? What if he was expelled and his wand was snapped in half? What would he do, where would he go? He could not return to living full-time with the Dursleys, *not now that he knew the other world, the one to which he really belonged*.[29]

During Harry's trial inside a secret room at Ministry headquarters, Headmaster Dumbledore makes a surprise appearance before the court and gives testimony in the boy's behalf. The result? Harry is cleared of all charges. Later that day:

It was starting to sink in: He was cleared, *he was going back to Hogwarts.*[30]

It took them twenty minutes to reach the King's Cross by foot and nothing more eventful happened during that time than Sirius scaring a couple of cats for Harry's entertainment. Once inside the station they lingered casually beside the barrier between platforms nine and ten until the coast was clear, then each of them leaned against it in turn and fell easily through onto platform nine and three quarters [sic.], where the Hogwarts Express stood belching sooty steam over a platform packed with departing students and their families. Harry inhaled the familiar smell and felt his spirits soar...*He was really going back....*[31]

Hidden within every human heart lies the need to belong. In Rowling's series, Harry feels this need inside the depths of his soul. There's nothing wrong with this. We all have it. As mentioned before, many of the themes within *Harry Potter* are universal. Harry is an orphan boy who misses his dad and mom. Kids can relate to this. Many readers are also fatherless or motherless in this cruel world of ours. The problem isn't that Harry Potter wants to belong. The core issue is, belong to what? Rowling's answer is unmistakable: *To the world of witchcraft.*

As we shall soon discover from the Holy Bible, *this is a problem.*

ENDNOTES

1. Ravenwolf, *Teen Witch*, pp. 5-6.
2. Rowling, *Sorcerer's Stone*, pp. 1-2.
3. Rowling, *Sorcerer's Stone*, p. 6.
4. Rowling, *Sorcerer's Stone*, p. 8.
5. Rowling, *Sorcerer's Stone*, pp. 13-14, 17.
6. Rowling, *Chamber of Secrets*, p. 3.
7. Rowling, *Chamber of Secrets*, p. 21.
8. Rowling, *Sorcerer's Stone*, p. 53.
9. Rowling, *Prisoner of Azkaban*, p. 31.

10. Rowling, *Chamber of Secrets*, p. 150.

11. Rowling, *Sorcerer's Stone*, p. 21.

12. Rowling, *Goblet of Fire*, pp. 26-27.

13. Rowling, *Sorcerer's Stone*, p. 50.

14. Rowling, *Goblet of Fire*, p. 20.

15. Rowling, *Chamber of Secrets*, p. 67.

16. Rowling, *Chamber of Secrets*, p. 38.

17. Rowling, *Prisoner of Azkaban*, pp. 1-3.

18. Rowling, *Chamber of Secrets*, p. 150.

19. Rowling, *Sorcerer's Stone*, pp. 102-103.

20. Rowling, *Chamber of Secrets*, p. 17.

21. Rowling, *Order of the Phoenix*, p. 467.

22. Rowling, *Chamber of Secrets*, p. 77.

23. Rowling, *Order of the Phoenix*, p. 616.

24. Rowling, *Goblet of Fire*, pp. 678-679.

25. Robert Frisken, of Christian Community Schools Ltd. in Australia, quoted in the *Sydney Morning Herald*, March 27, 2001.

26. Rowling, *Chamber of Secrets*, p. 16, italics added.

27. Rowling, *Order of the Phoenix*, p. 7, italics added.

28. Rowling, *Order of the Phoenix*, p. 37.

29. Rowling, *Order of the Phoenix*, p. 44, italics added.

30. Rowling, *Order of the Phoenix*, p. 153, italics added.

31. Rowling, *Order of the Phoenix*, pp. 181-182, italics added.

CHAPTER 9

THE ENEMY:
He-Who-Should-Be-Named

The first sin in our universe was Lucifer's self conceit.
—Thomas Carlyle (1795-1881)
Scottish Philosopher, Author

J.K. Rowling and *Harry Potter* fans generally believe that the classic conflict between good and evil that is raging on Planet Earth is being appropriately illustrated through the *Harry Potter* story. The "good" is represented by an orphaned wizard-boy who fights against evil—"the greatest sorcerer in the world"[1]—Lord Voldemort, a frightening being whose face is "flat and snakelike, with gleaming red eyes."[2] Voldemort is so wicked that friends and foes fear to speak his name. He's called "You Know Who," or "He-Who-Cannot-Be-Named."

Obviously, Voldemort doesn't exist, *but real evil does.* Where did it originate? What is its source? Can we understand its nature so we can detect its subtle disguises, resist its power, and even conquer its malicious strength? Yes, but *only* if we're willing to accept the teachings of the world's best-selling book—not *Harry Potter*, but the Bible. This point cannot be overemphasized. *The Word of God*, that's the key.

As a Christian author and parent with a keen interest in the *Harry Potter* controversy, I've been interviewed on many radio shows, both

Christian and secular, across the United States and Canada. On-the-air hosts often say things like, "What do you think of the *Harry Potter* books? Are they good or bad? Do they influence kids toward witchcraft? The lines are open! Give us a call at 1-800-...." Believe me, these shows then buzz with opinions as teenagers, parents, Christians, non-Christians, *Potter*-lovers, *Potter*-haters, and even Wiccans themselves grab their cell phones to inject their two cents worth. Many say, "They [*Potter* books] don't lead to real witchcraft, they're just fiction. Lighten up!" Others reply, "I'm not taking any chances. My child will *not* be reading those books!"

In the midst of heated discussion, I often interject this key question: "Do you believe what the Bible says about evil?" If they say, "No," then it's almost impossible to convince them of any potential "menace behind the magic." However, if they say, "Yes, one hundred percent!" then we have something to talk about.

It's not my purpose here to *prove* that the Bible is true (although I will give strong evidence in a later chapter). Obviously, the choice is yours. Yet I sincerely hope that as I reveal what God's Book really teaches about the mysterious origin of evil, that at least your heart will be open to "Consider what I say, and may the Lord give you understanding in all things" (2 Tim. 2:7).

We need to grasp the big picture to see the forest through the trees. Innumerable eons ago, reports the "Scripture of Truth" (Dan. 10:21)—even before the Great Creator made Planet Earth and human beings upon it—the Mighty God decided to make a network of intelligent and powerful beings called *angels* to inhabit His universe. Believe it or not, the only way to fully comprehend the issues within *Harry Potter*, the deeper issues of why evil exists, what its true nature is, and who started it, is to accept this fundamental biblical teaching: *Angels exist.*

The writer of the Book of Revelation declared:

Then I looked, and I heard the voice of many angels around the throne, the living creatures, and the elders; and the number of them was ten thousand times ten thousand, and thousands of thousands (Revelation 5:11).

Do the math. That's 100 million, plus thousands of thousands. We don't know the exact count, but it was a lot, and each of these angels was perfect, happy, loyal to God—and quite smart. Chances are they all had different names and knew each other. In any event, the Bible tells us one of them was named *lucifer*, meaning "light bearer," and indications are that he was the highest of them all. He was "the seal of perfection, full of wisdom and perfect in beauty" (Ezek. 28:12). Lucifer and his angelic associates were not only close friends, but they loved each other (for "God is love," 1 John 4:8); and all angels were content to reflect this love like sunlight as they sped throughout illimitable space.

That is, for a while. Mysteriously—it's unexplainable—lucifer became dissatisfied with his angelic position. God later declared through His prophet Isaiah:

How you are fallen from heaven, O Lucifer, son of the morning! How you are cut down to the ground, you who weakened the nations! For you have said in your heart: "I will ascend into heaven, I will exalt my throne above the stars of God; I will also sit upon the mount of the congregation, on the farthest sides of the north; I will ascend above the heights of the clouds, I will be like the Most High" (Isaiah 14:12-14).

God also spoke through Ezekiel of lucifer's exalted position and the mysterious process by which this mighty angel apostatized from his Maker, declaring:

You were the anointed cherub who covers; I established you; you were on the holy mountain of God; you walked back and forth in the midst of the fiery stones. You were perfect in your ways from the day you were created, till iniquity was found in you.... Your heart was lifted up because of your beauty; you

corrupted your wisdom for the sake of your splendor...
(Ezekiel 28:14-15,17).

There's no question that Ezekiel's words describe the apostasy of a non-human entity. He was "the anointed cherub who covers." Let me explain. In ancient times, the Israelites were instructed by God to build a temple that contained a special room called the Most Holy Place. Inside that hidden chamber was a golden box called "the ark of the covenant" (symbolizing God's throne), which had a golden lid on it called the Mercy Seat (illustrating the union of Justice and Mercy) upon which stood two golden statues of angelic beings called "cherubim" (see Exod. 37:7). The cherubim's wings were positioned to "cover" part of the Mercy Seat under which lay "the tables of the covenant"—stone tablets upon which were inscribed the Ten Commandments (see Heb. 9:3-5). *Lucifer was one of these covering angels!* This not only reveals that he held a very high position within God's government, but also that one of his probable assignments was to protect God's Law—a Law which expressed the eternal principles of His rule.

God told lucifer, "You were perfect in your ways from the day you were created, till iniquity was found in you" (Ezek. 28:15). Again, this cannot apply to any human being—only to an angel. Lucifer was "perfect" until "iniquity" was found in him. Like Isaiah before him, Ezekiel also pinpointed this mighty angel's core problem. *It was pride.*

Your heart was lifted up *because of your beauty; you corrupted your wisdom for the sake of your splendor...* (Ezekiel 28:17).

Deep inside lucifer's angelic personality—which we could call his "Chamber of Secrets"—his "heart was lifted up" against his Maker. Unexplainably, the shiny one began thinking too highly of himself. In a nutshell, lucifer yielded to a never-before-experienced desire for *self-exaltation* instead of maintaining a humble and focused passion *to exalt God.* The Almighty responded with this pointed verdict: "You sinned" (Ezek. 28:16).

Those two words, "you sinned," reveal what lucifer did from *God's perspective.* "Sin" is rebellion against the legitimate authority of God Himself as Supreme Creator of Heaven and earth. It is an inexcusable rejection of His Law; an uncalled-for challenge to His sovereignty. In other words, because God is the Source of life—including that of angels and humans—He has a valid right to be worshiped, honored, reverenced, and obeyed as Number One. And such obedience shouldn't be forced or grudgingly given, but willingly offered by all created beings because they *deeply appreciate* the Lord for who He is—the loving, unselfish, wondrous Source of all life.

"You sinned." That's how it started. Lucifer sinned by turning inward, by exalting himself, by seeking to reflect self instead of his Maker. Looking deeper, lucifer really desired to take God's place; the creature aspired to become Creator. The Lord's all-discerning eye penetrated the core of lucifer's being and saw what this mighty angel really wanted. It was power—*self power*—above God Almighty. This is how a perfect angel named lucifer, the light bearer, lost his brightness and enveloped himself in darkness.

Did the Lord try to save him? I'm sure He did. Because "God is love" (1 John 4:8), He surely loved lucifer, too. After all, He made him. Like a father yearns for his son or daughter, God must have experienced deep longings to rescue His shiny defector from misery and ruin. "Come now, and let us reason together" (Isa. 1:18), the Lord must have pleaded. Why not? God pleads with men, so wouldn't He have pleaded with His angels, too? It's logical.

But lucifer wouldn't yield his pride. As a result, he lost Heaven. Right after saying, "You sinned," the Lord continued. "Therefore I cast you as a profane thing out of the mountain of God" (Ezek. 28:16). The Book of Revelation says the same thing, yet inserts: "*his angels* were cast out with him" (Rev. 12:9). Those seven words—"his angels were cast out with him"—clearly imply that before lucifer was banished from Heaven he must have done some highly deceptive PR work among the other angels on behalf of his cause. And because Revelation teaches that there are still many loyal angels surrounding God's throne (Remember those 100 million still up there?), this implies that *every* angel must have been given a choice whom to serve—the Creator or the creature.

Lucifer must have presented arguments that seemed very convincing. Don't forget, we're talking about perfect angelic beings with brilliant minds. We're also talking about God Himself appealing directly to the entire angelic family with the facts about who created them in the first place. Here lies a sober truth: The devil is a highly intelligent, unbelievably subtle, and dangerously deceptive personality whose reasoning can even appear correct unless we believe God's Word. The rebel angel presented his case; God presented His. Eventually, every angel in heaven (millions and millions of them) took sides *for or against God.*

The Lord finally gave lucifer a new name. It wasn't a nice, friendly name—like one a loving parent gives a child. It was cold, dark, and foreboding. God's most brilliant angel had turned incorrigibly against Him, and had even deceived countless other angels into supporting his rebellious cause. So his name was switched to satan, meaning "adversary." It must have broken God's heart.

Why didn't God eliminate satan immediately? Wouldn't that have prevented untold damage? Enlightened reflection reveals a sensible answer. Satan's sin hadn't yet manifested itself as wholly destructive, even in front of the loyal angels (who at that point simply trusted what God told them). Satan probably asserted that he was seeking to *improve* Heaven's order, not overthrow it. He may have argued, "Hear ye, my angelic friends! Following *your will* is more beneficial than following *only God's will.* Trust me. See, I'm doing it and am enjoying great benefits!" Many angels were hoodwinked, while others didn't buy it—yet none of them had personally seen the disastrous results of proud selfishness. Not yet.

Here's a key point: Satan must have said his own way was "good," while the Lord's was "evil." This is the very nature of sin—it always justifies itself, defends itself, and calls itself good when it's really bad. Thus satan, bending his brilliant mind toward delusion, reversed the definitions. *He said evil was good and good was evil.* Such was the subtle nature of his deception, and he even seduced a sizable group of sinless angels to join his cause. But the Lord knew the truth. He knew that following His will was good, and that self-will was evil. Yet even His loyal angels couldn't fully see it, yet. That's why God gave lucifer time to play his hand—to show his true colors *as a devil in disguise.*

The Book of Revelation says a cosmic battle erupted between lucifer and his rebel angels (those who believed his lies) against God and His loyal angels (those who trusted their Maker's voice, even without visible evidence):

> *And war broke out in heaven: Michael and his angels fought with the dragon; and the dragon and his angels fought, but they [the rebel angels] did not prevail, nor was a place found for them in heaven any longer. So the great dragon was cast out, that serpent of old, called the Devil and Satan, who deceives the whole world;* **he was cast to the earth, and his angels were cast out with him** (Revelation 12:7-9).

This passage reveals that a mighty conflict is now raging! It started "in Heaven" and was transferred "to the earth." Satan lost the first war in Heaven, and he and his angelic sympathizers were forced out. Now he resides here on Planet Earth—he must have a headquarters somewhere—from which he operates to "deceive the whole world." In Heaven, satan deceived sinless angels; on earth, he deceives sinful men. His strategy is the same. He seeks to reverse humanity's perception of the essentials of the Creator/creature relationship by convincing people that self-will is good, positive, and beneficial, and that following God's will is evil, negative, and harmful—or at least not too smart.

Chronologically, it was sometime after satan's expulsion from Heaven that this Scripture was fulfilled: "In the beginning God created the heavens and the earth" (Gen. 1:1). This is the first verse in the Bible, and it teaches this fundamental truth: God Almighty is the Creator of Planet Earth. According to Genesis chapters 1 and 2, God made the light (first day), our atmosphere (second day), the earth (third day), the sun, moon, and stars (fourth day), the animals, birds, and sea creatures (fifth day), Adam and Eve (sixth day), and "He rested on the seventh day from all His work which He had done" (Gen. 2:2).

Human beings were the crowning act of God's creativity, as it is written:

> *Then God said, "Let Us make man in Our image, according to Our likeness: let them have dominion over the fish of the sea, over the birds of the air, over the cattle, over all the earth and over every creeping thing that creeps upon the earth." So God created man in His own image: in the image of God He created Him; male and female He created them* (Genesis 1:26-27).

In "the image of God" means that humankind was uniquely designed to reflect the love, truthfulness, and goodness of their Creator. Contrary to modern psycho-theories, we weren't created primarily to develop good *self*-images, but to experience happiness and contentment through reflecting *His* image. And this blessed God-reflection can only be maintained by trusting our Creator, submitting to His will, and by obeying His Law (principles), believing He knows what's best.

God spared nothing to make Adam and Eve happy. He even planted an exotic garden for them to live in, as it is written: "The Lord God planted a garden eastward in Eden, and there He put the man whom He had formed" (Gen. 2:8).

Of course He knew about the Great Rebellion and the malicious determination of the light-bearer-now-adversary to usurp dominion over His perfect new world. He also knew that just as He offered heavenly angels a choice to serve Him or not, the same freedom must be given to man. "God is love" (1 John 4:8); love involves freedom, freedom requires choice, and choice necessitates risk. God doesn't want robots, but relationships. So, He grants freedom, even to the devil. There's no other way.

In His perfect wisdom, God decided to create a test—a tree at which man could either prove his loyalty, or rebel.

> *And out of the ground the Lord God made every tree grow that is pleasant to the sight and good for food. The tree of life was also in the midst of the garden, **and the tree of the knowledge of good and evil*** (Genesis 2:9).

Apparently, satan and his angelic fiends (also called "demons," "devils," or "evil spirits" in the Bible) were only allowed access to the thoughts of Adam and Eve at "the tree of the knowledge of good and evil." That was the place where the sinless couple would be tempted to choose another master. Adam wasn't left without warning. Because the Creator loved His new son, He spoke directly, earnestly, and ever-so-clearly to avoid any possible confusion:

> *And the Lord God commanded the man, saying, "Of every tree of the garden you may freely eat: but of the tree of the knowledge of good and evil you shall not eat, for in the day that you eat from it you shall surely die"* (Genesis 2:16-17).

"Of every tree of the garden you may *freely* eat" reveals that God had given Adam and Eve great freedom. He isn't a tyrant or dictator, but a loving Father who wants relationships with His children. An entire garden filled with delicious fruit lay at Adam and Eve's feet. They were *free* to eat peaches, plums, watermelons, figs, grapes, and apricots filled with juicy flavors we can hardly imagine. There were no restrictions—except one. One tree involved a test, a choice. The issue was life or death.

The restricted tree was called "the tree of the knowledge of good and evil." Evidently, God knew that satan's strategy was not only to reverse reality by calling evil good and good evil, but to also go a step farther—he would mix good and evil elements together *to deceive.* Smart devil! Remember, lucifer's no dummy. But God *never* mixes good with evil, or truth with error. He only creates and promotes perfect goodness. And that's what He commands us to choose, *always*. He doesn't compromise.

Significantly, after each creative day recorded in Genesis 1, the Lord saw His handiwork and said, "it was good" (see Gen. 1:4,10,12, 18,21,25). Finally, at the conclusion of creation week, "God saw everything He had made, and indeed *it was* **very good**" (Gen. 1:31). Thus God is the Author of good only, and after creating man "in His image," He wanted *only good* for man. As long as man chose good only—which means obeying God fully—he was safe. Notice also that "the tree of the knowledge of good and evil" was *entirely forbidden*. Curiosity must be restrained. "If you take even one bite from its fruit, that's it, *you will surely die!*" warned the Lord.

In Genesis 3, the drama begins:

Now the serpent was more cunning than any beast of the field which the Lord God had made. And he said to the woman... (Genesis 3:1).

"The serpent" was a creature God made. Of itself, it wasn't cunning, for it was just a reptile. It was really the rebel angel—who slipped inside the serpent—who was the cunning one. It is interesting to note that this particular snake now has the infamous honor of being the very first medium in human history. That beady-eyed creature became "a channel" for another mind to utter its satanic thoughts through its serpent brain. It's also important to realize that when satan spoke to Eve, she *wasn't aware* that she was listening to a separate, non-reptilian intelligence. But she was. That's why God called the snake "more cunning."

And he [the serpent] *said to the woman, "Has God indeed said, 'You shall not eat of every tree of the garden?'"* (Genesis 3:1)

Clever question indeed! Essentially, satan was implying that God was a freedom-limiter, not a freedom-giver. By questioning whether the Lord was restricting Adam and Eve from enjoying *every* tree—God had only forbidden one—satan was really challenging God's goodness, fairness, and unselfishness, whether He knew what was best for His creatures. This was the same challenge lucifer whispered around Heaven. Satan didn't just want freedom up yonder, but *unrestricted* freedom to do as he jolly well pleased. God told him, "You can't do that. I know what's best." "I'm not sure about that," shot back the rebel angel. That's why he had to go. The exact same challenge was presented to Adam's wife.

Eve took the bait and made her first mistake—she dialoged with an entity whose IQ is possibly one billion:

> *And the woman said to the serpent, "We may eat of the fruit of the trees of the garden; but of the fruit of the tree which is in the midst of the garden, God has said, 'You shall not eat, nor shall you touch it, lest you die'"* (Genesis 3:2-3).

Eve clarified that her Creator had granted them freedom to eat fruit from all "the trees of the garden," except one; the one, coincidentally, that the talking snake just happened to be slithering around in. Eve then affirmed that disobedience to that solitary, reasonable restriction merited the death penalty. Satan countered:

> *Then the serpent said to the woman, "You will not surely die. For God knows that in the day you eat of it your eyes will be opened, and you will be like God, knowing good and evil"* (Genesis 3:4-5).

Note carefully the lies of the devil. Satan's exact lines to Eve were:

1. "You will not surely die."
2. "Your eyes will be opened."
3. "You will be like God."
4. "Knowing good and evil"

His diabolically deceptive implications were:

1. God is wrong.

2. Death is not the result of sin.

3. Eating the forbidden fruit brings enlightenment.

4. Eve could become a little god herself.

5. Mixing good and evil is beneficial.

6. Start nibbling—it's good for you!

Eve stood motionless as two voices battled inside her brain and the entire universe stared breathlessly from beyond the stars. One voice pleaded, "Don't do it. Be content. Obey. Let God be God!" The other chided, "Don't believe it. You'll never be happy until *you become god yourself*, knowing good and evil."

Eve's decision would be manifested in the tiniest act—eating or not eating. It was obedience versus disobedience, loyalty versus rebellion, trusting the Source of life versus believing the father of lies. As Eve pondered conflicting choices, humanity's future trembled in the balance. What should she do? Should she be satisfied with being just a creature, reflecting God's image, and avoiding what God said to avoid? Or should she pluck the forbidden fruit, seek freedom apart from her Creator, and enter the path of trying to *reflect her own image*? Distilling things down to the bare essentials, the core issue was: God's power or Eve's power, God's will or Eve's will; *self or the Lord*? You know what happened. Paul later wrote, "the woman being deceived, fell into transgression" (1 Tim. 2:14). Eve was duped. She "transgressed" against the Word, Will, and Law of the Supreme Governor of the Universe. Even more than this: Her sin pierced His loving heart.

> *So when the woman saw that the tree was good for food, that it was pleasant to the eyes, and a tree desirable to make one wise, she took of its fruit and ate...* (Genesis 3:6).

Notice carefully: After dialoging with the snake, Eve suddenly "saw" the forbidden fruit as "good for food" and desirable for wisdom. It was nothing of the sort! But satanic thoughts were now rolling around inside her pretty head. Now she "saw" things in reverse! What was blatantly evil, she perceived as good, and what was truly good (doing God's will), she thought was evil. That's what sin does—it blinds the mind and causes it to see from satan's backward perspective.

...she took of its fruit and ate (Genesis 3:6).

Eve's tiny act sent shock waves throughout the universe. But that wasn't all...

She also gave to her husband with her... (Genesis 3:6b).

That's the nature of sin. Once *you* do it, you want *others* to do it. The same thing happened in Heaven. As soon as lucifer became a devil he began campaigning to make all of his angelic friends into devils. So it was with Eve. As soon as she sinned by tasting the forbidden fruit, she hastened to make Adam a sinner, too.

This leads to another vital point: When Eve first dialoged with the talking reptile, she was totally unaware that there was a malicious presence working *through it*. Similarly, when she offered the fruit to Adam, she was also unconscious that the very same diabolical entity was now inside humanity working *through her!* Eve had become a channel of temptation herself—an agent of death to the one she loved most, her husband, Adam. Did she know it? No. Thus a person can become a "channel" for satan without knowing it. As Paul later wrote, satan is "the spirit who now works *in* the sons of disobedience" (Eph. 2:2).

She also gave to her husband with her, and he ate (Genesis 3:6b).

Loyal angels wept. They could hardly believe it. Adam and Eve had chosen lucifer, just as millions of their former angelic friends had done! And just like the consequences for fallen angels were not what they supposed—they were kicked out of Heaven—even so the unexpected results were swift on earth. Instead of reaping happiness, freedom, and mini-godhood as the serpent promised, the opposite occurred:

Then the eyes of both of them were opened, and they knew that they were naked; and they sewed fig leaves together and made themselves coverings (Genesis 3:7).

When Adam and Eve tasted the forbidden fruit, their eyes were opened indeed; but instead of spiritual illumination, "they knew that they were naked." Instead of happiness, a chilling sense of guilt crept over them. Instead of limitless freedom, they began experiencing the bondage of a captured-by-sin, God-empty soul. Too late, too late! They learned you can't trust the devil. A few hours later:

> *...they heard the sound of the Lord God walking in the garden in the cool of the day, and Adam and his wife hid themselves from the presence of the Lord God among the trees of the garden. Then the Lord God called to Adam and said to him, "Where are you?" So he* [Adam] *said, "I heard Your voice in the garden, and I was afraid because I was naked; and I hid myself"* (Genesis 3:8-10).

People have been hiding from "the presence of the Lord" ever since. They know not "[His] voice in the garden." "I was afraid," Adam moaned, "because I was naked." It's the same today. Fear grips Planet Earth, yet few understand the reason why. The root cause is one deadly word: SIN. God told lucifer in Heaven, "You sinned" (Ezek. 28:16). His Word further identifies "the angels who sinned" (2 Pet. 2:4). Because of Eve's disastrous choice to pluck the forbidden fruit, "Sin entered the world, and death through sin, and thus death spread to all men, because all sinned" (Rom. 5:12).

Because Adam and Eve chose the way of the snake, the "war in Heaven" was transferred to earth, plunging our first parents—and all their descendants—into an ongoing, life-and-death, vicious struggle between God and His loyal angels against lucifer's legions.

How can we win this war? In our own strength, we can't. We're no match for the powerful forces of satan and his invisible fallen entities. But the Good News is that Heaven has instituted a special plan—I call it "Operation Rescue Sinners"—which we'll study more soon. But at this point, we must begin where Adam and Eve failed. We must start by listening carefully to an ancient language, to "[His] voice in the garden," to the Word of our loving Heavenly Father who knows what's best for us; the voice our first parents chose to ignore.

In the next chapter we'll discover that the exact same voice which lovingly yet earnestly warned against tasting the forbidden fruit also warns about deadly occult practices (like witchcraft, sorcery, potions, and spells). That same heavenly voice cautions us about being deceived by people who sincerely yet unknowingly are channels for satan's thoughts, and about making the same mistake lucifer, many angels, and Eve made—that of reversing reality and thinking evil is good and good is evil.

Will we listen to His voice?

ENDNOTES

1. Rowling, *Sorcerer's Stone*, p. 57.
2. Rowling, *Goblet of Fire*, p. 640.

CHAPTER 10

THE CURSE:

What the Bible Says About Sorcery

Pure truth cannot be assimilated by the crowd.
—Henri Frederic Amiel (1821-1881)
Swiss Philosopher, Poet

The Bible accurately records the course of human history from the creation of Planet Earth to the end of time. It reveals the inexcusable and disastrous fall of Adam and Eve, the ongoing conflict between good and evil, Operation Rescue Sinners (more on this later), and the ultimate triumph of God's love, goodness, and truth over the sneaky delusions of the master trickster—the fallen angel who spoke through the snake.

Ever since our first parents tasted the forbidden fruit, fallen, lost, bewildered, mixed-up humans have sought that elusive sense of peace originally lost in the Garden of Eden. Throughout history different religions, systems, philosophies, theologies, and psychologies have offered opinions about our human condition and tried to supply what vanished in Paradise. Unfortunately, most have failed miserably because they don't understand, or else they refuse to accept, the basic truths about our Creator, sin, obedience, and the subtle workings of the rebel angel. The sober reality is that just as lucifer spoke through a reptile and then through Eve, he's also spoken through countless teachers, scientists, philosophers, theologians, and even misguided authors who are "ignorant of his devices" (2 Cor. 2:11).

Although the message of this book applies to every area of life, its targeted focus is one particular track of delusion: witchcraft and sorcery. J.K. Rowling's first book, *Harry Potter and the Sorcerer's Stone*, didn't come off the press until 1998, yet the practices mentioned therein—witchcraft, sorcery, potions, spells, and divination—have been around for ages. These exact words are in the Bible, and they've been sitting there for thousands of years.

It's time to discover what the Holy Scriptures teach about these things. Believe me, it is eye-opening. We'll start with Exodus, Leviticus, and Deuteronomy, and will finish with Revelation. But before we look at any witchcraft passages, notice carefully this short but illuminating verse in the Psalms. Talking to God, King David said:

For with You is the fountain of life; in Your light we see light (Psalm 36:9).

David called God "the fountain of life." As we've already seen, life originated from our loving Creator. He's the Supreme Source of everything that breathes. Look closely at these six words in the second half of the verse, "*in Your light we see light.*" They reveal the penetrating fact that it's only through *God's light* that we are enabled to "see light." Remember how Eve *thought* she saw light, but saw darkness? Her blindness resulted from her rejection of God's voice. In other words, God's voice is the source of correct thinking. David clarified in another Psalm, "Your word is a lamp to my feet and a light to my path" (Ps. 119:105). To summarize: If we accept God's Word, we'll "see light" and understand truth from *His perspective.*

Everyone knows the *Harry Potter* novels are saturated with occult references to "witches," "wizards," "sorcery," and "spells"—with "good" witches often portrayed in a humorous and friendly light. Yet these witchy words are never so presented in the Bible. When we look at what God's Book says about these things, we learn what He thinks—from His perspective. Prepare yourself, for you are about to hear God's voice. As you do, I sincerely hope that *"in His light you shall see light."* May the Lord help us to perceive through Spirit-enlightened eyes how deathly serious this topic is. It isn't child's play.

Approximately 2,600 years after Adam and Eve plucked the forbidden fruit, God rescued over 1 million persons from Egyptian slavery. Remember Moses? Ten plagues on Pharaoh? Blood on the doors? The Passover? These things occurred in history when the Lord set Israel free. As the newly delivered nation meandered through a barren wilderness toward the Promised Land, God spoke explicit instructions through Moses. Some of it concerned witchcraft. The Great Deliverer said:

> *You shall not permit a sorceress to live* (Exodus 22:18).

> *Regard not them that have familiar spirits, neither seek after wizards, to be defiled by them: I am the Lord your God* (Leviticus 19:31 KJV).

> *A man also or woman that hath a familiar spirit, or is a wizard, shall surely be put to death: they shall stone them with stones: their blood shall be upon them* (Leviticus 20:27 KJV).

"Neither seek after wizards, to be defiled by them," the Almighty thundered. All sorcerers must be executed; their blood is upon them. And notice that the Bible doesn't differentiate between "good" and "evil" sorcerers. *Anyone* who is a "wizard" must "be put to death." Strong words; too strong for many. Yet the Lord has His reasons for stating them, *and they're good ones*. Later we'll look closer at *how* wizards defile and *why* God said these things. But for now, it's enough to discover the verses themselves.

Shortly after Leviticus is Deuteronomy, the fifth book in the Bible. As I think of Moses' fifth book—especially chapter 18—I can't help thinking about fifth-year students at Hogwarts studying for their O.W.L. exams. It's too bad Harry Potter, Ron Weasley, and Hermione Granger didn't memorize Deuteronomy 18 as part of their test preparation. If they did, Hogwarts might change its curriculum.

Notice the comprehensiveness of God's counsel to His ancient people:

> *When you come into the land which the Lord your God is giving you, you shall not learn to follow the abominations of those nations. There shall not be found among you anyone who makes his son or his daughter pass through the fire, or one who practices witchcraft, or a soothsayer, or one who interprets omens, or a sorcerer, or one who conjures spells, or a medium, or a spiritist, or one who calls up the dead. For all who do these things are an abomination to the Lord, and because of these abominations the Lord your God drives them out from before you. You shall be blameless before the Lord your God* (Deuteronomy 18:9-13).

Here God warns against "witchcraft," becoming "a sorcerer," casting "spells," and communication with "the dead." *This is exactly what the Harry Potter books are about.* Hogwarts, Hagrid, Dumbledore, and Voldemort's Death Eaters may be fictitious, yet these occult activities surely aren't. They've been practiced for centuries among the "nations." And again, there's no distinction made between white witches who cast good spells (like Harry Potter and Albus Dumbledore) and dark wizards (like Voldemort) who conjure nasty ones. No, "witchcraft" and "spells" are entirely forbidden, and "*all* who do these things are an abomination to the Lord."

In Rowling's series, all students at Hogwarts School of Witchcraft and Wizardry are required to take classes on Potions, Spells, and Divination, just like real kids take Mathematics, History, English, or Algebra. Yet God commands us to avoid these evil practices entirely. "You shall *not learn*" about them, says the Lord. Yet J.K. Rowling and her publisher (Scholastic, Inc.) defend themselves with this disclaimer:

"Don't worry, it's just fiction." Yet as we've seen, it's not all "just fiction"—there's plenty of real stuff within those pages.

From a biblical perspective, here are deeper questions: Are Joanne Kathleen Rowling and Scholastic, Inc. *unknowingly* being used by the same entity that deceived perfect angels and spoke lies through the snake? In the *Potter* books, is what God calls evil being viewed as good? All who respect God's voice in His Book should consider these sober questions. Remember, satan and his fallen angelic hosts "deceive the whole world" (Rev. 12:9). It's no joke.

Again, while much of *Harry Potter* is funny and fictitious, these exact words—"witchcraft," "sorcery," "potions," "spells," and "divination"—are associated with non-fictitious practices performed by real witches throughout human history, including biblical history. And as Silver Ravenwolf's *Teen Witch: Wicca for a New Generation* plainly shows, modern devotees of the Craft are *doing them now*. All of these witchy words evoke a sense of mystery and are fascinating to teenagers, which contributes greatly to Pottermania. Yet they're strictly, totally, categorically, and unequivocally forbidden in God's Word, just like the forbidden fruit. Albus Dumbledore told Harry Potter, "Curiosity is not a sin." True; nevertheless, curiosity about what God has strictly forbidden can lead to sin and death. Ask Eve. Consider God's Word and "His light." *This applies to witchcraft.*

In spite of the fictitious elements—and regardless of what *Potter* supporters naively claim—kids *are* learning about occult mysteries and history when they read about Professor Binn's History of Magic class (remember "Witch Burnings...discuss"?), Professor Snape's Potions class, Professor Flitwick's Charms class, Professor Trelawney's Divination class (she "channeled" Voldemort's spirit), and the Restricted Section in Hogwarts library containing Dark Arts books. Yet most parents aren't worried because "Johnny's reading a book," the novels are funny, contain some good lessons, and are even being incorporated into the U.S. public school system as appropriate conveyors of "values." Yet most have no clue there's a tricky devil on the loose, especially since these same public schools don't allow the reading of the Bible in the classroom. He-who-should-be-named must be quite pleased.

Next book of the Bible: First Samuel. Samuel was an ancient prophet who respected God's voice. After King Saul failed to carry out some specific instructions commanded by the Lord, Samuel moaned with agonizing remorse:

> *"Has the Lord as great delight in burnt offerings and sacrifices, as in obeying the voice of the Lord? Behold, to obey is better than sacrifice, and to heed than the fat of rams. For rebellion is as* **the sin of witchcraft***, and stubbornness is as the iniquity and idolatry. Because you have rejected the word of the Lord, He has also rejected you from being king." Then Saul said to Samuel, "I have sinned, for I have transgressed the commandment of the Lord and your words, because I feared the people and obeyed their voice"* (1 Samuel 15:22-24).

This passage is full of instruction. Witchcraft itself is called a "sin" (more on this later) and is associated with rebellion, stubbornness, and idolatry. Sounds like what happened in Heaven, doesn't it? King Saul "rejected the word of the Lord"—just like lucifer, many angels, and Adam and Eve. Saul finally admitted that he sinned because he "feared the people and obeyed their voice," instead of his Maker's voice. Today *Harry Potter* is popular among "the people," yet someone once said, "What is popular is not always right, and what is right is not always popular." Think about it: Can the same God who warned against "the sin of witchcraft" be pleased today with a series of books and movies that make what He so firmly condemned in ancient times now appear fun for kids? I don't think so. Especially when *real* witchcraft is becoming an "In" thing among teenagers!

Let's move to Second Chronicles. Manasseh, one of Israel's most wicked rulers, "reigned fifty-five years in Jerusalem" (2 Chron. 33:1). Yet just like King Saul, he also rejected the Lord's word. The Bible elaborates upon his sins:

*Also he caused his sons to pass through the fire in the Valley
of the Son of Hinnom; he practiced soothsaying, used witchcraft and sorcery, and consulted mediums and spiritists. He
did much evil in the sight of the Lord, to provoke Him to
anger* (2 Chronicles 33:6).

Not a pretty picture. But now, instead of these practices occurring
only among "the nations" outside of Israel, they've slipped into God's
camp and are being performed by one of their own kings. And don't
miss the fact that when Manasseh "used witchcraft and sorcery" he
"did much evil in the sight of the Lord." Here's a key question: Did
Manasseh do wrong simply because he "*used* witchcraft and sorcery,"
or because he *misused* a positive art for evil purposes? In other words,
is witchcraft inherently a nasty thing "in the sight of the Lord," or is it
a neutral science, capable of being used either way—for good or evil—
depending on the intent of the user?

This question is highly relevant because in the *Harry Potter*
books, the Walt Disney-sponsored *W.I.T.C.H.* series, the popular
Charmed novels, the page-turning *Daughters of the Moon* series, Silver Ravenwolf's *Teen Witch* book, and in countless other movies, TV
shows, witchy games, and non-fiction Wiccan works, witchcraft is almost always presented as a positive science capable of being used for
"good" purposes—that's its appeal. Which is it? If you ask most Wiccans, they'll invariably say, "Witchcraft can be used for good or evil.
It's up to the witch."

Best-selling Wiccan author Scott Cunningham, in his popular pro-
witchcraft book, *The Truth About Witchcraft Today*, clearly promotes
this as a core doctrine of the Craft. Notice carefully:

The power at work in folk magic is just that—power. It is neither positive nor negative, neither good nor evil. It is the in-
tention and goal of the magician working with it that
determines whether this energy is used for helpful or harmful ends.[1]

This is Wiccan philosophy; but the Bible teaches something different. Look again: Manasseh "*used* witchcraft and sorcery;" there's nothing said about misusing it. He also did "much evil *in the sight of the Lord*" (2 Chron. 33:6). The phrase "in the sight of the Lord" contains the key to knowledge. As we've already seen, the truest definition of what's good or evil depends on God's perspective, not man's. In Holy Scripture, whether something is good or evil is inseparably intertwined with how created beings relate to their Creator. God's Word also reveals that fallen beings—both human and angelic—are quite capable of skewed perceptions and seeing things backwards. That's why Isaiah warned:

> *Woe to those who call evil good, and good evil; who put darkness for light, and light for darkness; who put bitter for sweet and sweet for bitter!* (Isaiah 5:20)

That's what sin does. It reverses reality in the minds of those duped by the devil. So let's reverse it back. Make no mistake about it: In God's Word, "witchcraft" *is evil*, not good, and a fearful "woe" is pronounced on those who distort the truth.

Advancing to the New Testament, we find many references to witchcraft and sorcery, and once again, they're all bad. Many are in the Book of Acts, which chronicles the Christian Church's growth in the first century right after Jesus Christ died for our sins and rose from the dead. As Paul was spreading the good news of a crucified and risen Savior throughout the Roman world, "Elymas the sorcerer" opposed him, "seeking to turn [others] away from the faith" (Acts 13:8).

> *Then Saul, who was also called Paul, filled with the Holy Spirit, looked intently at him and said, "O full of all deceit and all fraud, you son of the devil, you enemy of all righteousness, will you not cease perverting the straight ways of the Lord? And now, indeed, the hand of the Lord is upon you, and you shall be blind, not seeing the sun for a time." And immediately a dark mist fell on him, and he went around seeking someone to lead him by the hand* (Acts 13:9-11).

Shocking, isn't it? Paul called Elymas the sorcerer a "son of the devil"! He was "full of all deceit" (witchcraft is deceptive), an "enemy of all righteousness" (his sorcery was wrong), who was "perverting the straight ways of the Lord" (God's way is straight). In other words, Elymas was a subtle channel for the rebel angel, just like the snake had become in the Garden of Eden. Many didn't discern this, but Paul did, because he was "filled with the Holy Spirit" and saw through Spirit-eyes. Not so with Elymas. At Paul's command, a supernatural darkness—like a cloudy mist—enveloped the sorcerer and his vision faded. This inky blackness reflected the mental blindness inside Elymas' brain.

A few chapters later a Spirit-led revival swept through the Greek coastal city of Ephesus, on the shores of Asia Minor (now modern Turkey), and "the name of the Lord Jesus was magnified" (Acts 19:17). As a result:

...many of those who had practiced magic brought their books together and burned them in the sight of all. And they counted up the value of them, and it totaled fifty thousand pieces of silver. So the word of the Lord grew mightily and prevailed (Acts 19:19-20).

Those citizens of Ephesus renounced their occult ways, cast their magic books into the flames, and believed in "the name of the Lord Jesus." Then "the word of the Lord grew mightily and prevailed."

Later, Paul wrote to Christians in the Roman Province of Galatia, outlining two paths before them—walking "in the Spirit" or following "the lusts of the flesh" (Gal. 5:16). Paul listed 17 "works of the flesh" and warned the Galatians that if they practiced them, the consequences would be disastrous. What are those works of the flesh? Notice carefully:

*Now the works of the flesh are evident, which are: adultery, fornication, uncleanness, lewdness, idolatry, **sorcery**, hatred, contentions, jealousies, outbursts of wrath, selfish ambitions, dissensions, heresies, envy, murders, drunkenness, revelries, and the like; of which I tell you beforehand, just as I have*

also told you in time past, that those who practice such things
will not inherit the kingdom of God (Galatians 5:19-21).

Sorcery is listed as one of "the works of the flesh." Once again,
there's nothing said about the *misuse* of sorcery. To Paul, sorcery itself
was a fleshy thing, and "those who practice such things will not inherit the kingdom of God." Not a good sign for Hogwarts.

Finally, we come to the Book of Revelation—the last and most
mysterious book in the Bible, containing prophecies about the future of
Planet Earth. Referring to those who persistently reject God's love and
mercy, the Scripture declares:

*And they did not repent of their murders or their **sorceries** or*
their sexual immorality or their thefts (Revelation 9:21).

But the cowardly, unbelieving, abominable, murderers, sexu-
*ally immoral, **sorcerers**, idolaters, and all liars shall have*
their part in the lake which burns with fire and brimstone,
which is the second death (Revelation 21:8).

*But outside are dogs and **sorcerers** and sexually immoral and*
murderers and idolaters, and whoever loves and practices a
lie (Revelation 22:15).

We must not take these verses lightly. Revelation places sorcerers
right next to those who "love and practice a lie." Along with murderers,
the sexually immoral, and idolaters, they are on a fast track toward "the
lake that burns with fire and brimstone, which is the second death."

Now you know what God's Word *really says* about "witches,"
"witchcraft," "wizards" "sorcery," "sorceries," "spells," and "divination." Unlike J.K. Rowling's *Harry Potter* novels, it describes *no* conflict between white and black witches; and all non-magical people are
certainly not classified as Muggles. Instead, it's *witchcraft against God*.
Exodus, Leviticus, Deuteronomy, First Samuel, Second Chronicles,
Acts, Galatians, and Revelation all say the same thing: Witchcraft is a
real, non-fictitious, satanically inspired, and highly deceptive "work of

the flesh," pleasantly charming its naïve practitioners toward burning flames and brimstone.

In the sober light of these anti-sorcery verses, perhaps you can understand why Scott Cunningham, in his pro-witchcraft book, *The Truth About Witchcraft*, inserts his own counter-warning to those exploring the Craft:

> Be especially careful when reading works that contain numerous Biblical quotations. They're filled with outright lies and inaccuracies.[2]

Here Scott Cunningham denies God's Word, just like the serpent did in Eden. Thus we've come full circle. Again, the fundamental issue is whether we trust the Bible or not. Mr. Cunningham—a practicing witch who thinks witchcraft is good—doesn't.

As for me, I'm a believer.

ENDNOTES

1. Scott Cunningham, *The Truth About Witchcraft Today* (St. Paul, MN: Llewellyn Publications, 2001), p. 39.

2. Scott Cunningham, *The Truth About Witchcraft* (St. Paul, MN: Llewellyn, 2002), p. 53.

CHAPTER 11

THE EVIDENCE:
Potter Fans Turn to Witchcraft

Any time the dark side of the supernatural world
is presented as harmless or even imaginary, there is
the danger that children will become curious and find out
too late that witchcraft is neither harmless nor imaginary.
—Lindy Beam, Focus on the Family[1]

I s Pottermania fueling Wiccan growth today? When I join radio shows to discuss this controversial question, *Potter* supporters often phone in and say, "Don't be silly. You're taking *Harry* too seriously." *Potter* critics dial in right behind them countering, "Haven't you read the Bible? I'm not letting my child read those books!"

One show was different; I remember it quite well. It was Friday, June 4, 2003, and I was a guest on the large CFRB 1020 FM station in Toronto, Canada. Four callers disagreed with me—which wasn't so unusual—yet three said something I hadn't heard before. They not only thought *Harry Potter* was innocent, but each took the next step by asking, "So what's wrong with Wicca anyway? It's a valid religion. I know some very nice people who practice it!" One man snarled, "Look at Church history! Christianity's the real problem—look at all the witch burnings!" Now, I don't justify witch burnings, and it's true that

Church history is filled with blunders. Big ones. Yet that particular interview demonstrated how the Wiccan religion is gaining wider acceptance in North America. That last comment even sounded a bit like the slant of those "reliable historical sources" Harry Potter learned about in Professor Binn's History of Magic class!

Again, *is Harry Potter fueling Wiccan growth today?* Most parents don't think so, including many Christian parents. Before attempting an answer, let me share a report from two friends of mine shortly after *Harry Potter and the Chamber of Secrets* hit theaters. Gospel singer, Christian Berdahl and his wife, Coby, took a video camera and microphone to Stadium 12 in Lodi, California, to interview those who had just viewed the movie as part of a documentary on *Harry Potter*. In a letter dated September 15, 2004, Mr. Berdahl described what happened:

> While videotape was rolling, Coby asked some questions of an upper middle class mother, her 12-year-old son and her 16-year-old daughter about the *Harry Potter* movie they had just seen.
>
> Coby: "Did you like the movie?"
> Son: "Oh, yeah it was cool."
> Daughter: "Yeah, cool."
> Mother: "It was fun......it was fine."
>
> Coby: "What did you like most about it?"
> Son: "All the magic and stuff......you could like get even and get back at people who you didn't like or something."
> Daughter: "Yeah, the magic......it would be cool to have powers like that."
>
> Coby: "What does mom think about all of this?"
> Mother: "Oh, it's fine and harmless fun for kids......I mean the books are great and my kids enjoy reading them. And they are both reading the same books and we are able to talk about them......so I like that."
>
> Coby: "If there was a real Hogwarts School would you want to go?"

Son: "Oh YEAH!! That would be so cool!
Daughter: "Yeah, I'd go too!"

Coby: "Since you have been reading about all this stuff, have you ever tried magic or learning spells?"

AT THE VERY SAME MOMENT!
Mother: "Oh NO!"
Daughter: "Yeah, I......"
Mother interrupting: "BETTER NOT!!!"

The daughter smiled and shrugged at Coby as the mother said, "Let's go!"

This is the account of one of the dozens of interviews we had that day...

In His Service,
Christian & Coby Berdahl
Lodi, CA

Christian later told me about other things that happened that day. A mother, son, and little 5-year-old daughter came out of the theater and were interviewed. The girl was in tears because the film was so scary. "Toughen up," the mom said. Christian and Coby also entered the theater and met the manager, said they were doing a documentary, and requested permission to take some footage. "Sure, let's go right into the movie room." As they entered before the house lights went down, the manager announced to those seated, "These people are doing a documentary on *Harry Potter*. If anyone wants to be interviewed, step right up." Quickly a line formed and kids starting screaming, "Yea! Harry Potter rules!" It was totally chaotic.

The theater manager later told Christian and Coby he had never seen such craziness over any film. He saw the movie himself and confessed, "It should never be shown to children." He also said one woman pre-purchased 12 tickets for her son's birthday (for the boy and his friends), but decided to preview the film first. After watching a portion, she walked out and begged for a refund, declaring, "My child will not be seeing this movie!"

Just to clarify: I'm not saying every teenager who reads a *Harry Potter* book or watches a *Potter* film will rush out to join a coven. Yet—as the mother-daughter interview at the theater showed—some kids are becoming interested in witchcraft through watching their hero perform supernatural feats with the flick of his wand. As impressionable as youth are, it's only natural. With eyes wide open, Robert Night of *The Family Research Council* warned that in the midst of the fun, fright, and magic, *Harry Potter* "gives children an appetite for the occult."[2]

If you want real evidence, here's some that's hard to ignore: The Pagan Federation is a well-organized promoter of Wicca witchcraft in England.[3] Shortly after J.K. Rowling's series became popular in the British Isles, the Federation started receiving "a flood of inquiries" about the details of their religion—inquiries they publicly attributed to "the success of the *Harry Potter* books."[4] A British publication, *This Is London*, reported the facts in an article bearing this sobering title: "Potter Fans Turning to Witchcraft." The Federation's media spokesman, Andy Norfolk, explained:

> In response to increased inquiries coming from youngsters we established a youth officer...It is quite probably linked to things like *Harry Potter*, *Sabrina the Teenage Witch* and *Buffy the Vampire Slayer*. Every time an article on witchcraft or paganism appears, we have a huge surge in calls, mostly from young girls.[5]

"Potter Fans Turning to Witchcraft," "the success of the Harry Potter books," "linked to things like Harry Potter," "a huge surge in calls, mostly from young girls"—these aren't minor sentences. And notice the connection between kids seeing witchcraft in the media and then wanting to do it. Hollywood producers know not what they do.

Moving beyond the report of the Pagan Federation, kids themselves have testified how *Harry Potter* draws them toward witchcraft and the occult:

"I like what they learned there [at Hogwarts] and I want to be a witch."

—Gioia Bishop, ten years old.[6]

"I thought the story really made you feel like you could be a witch or a wizard."

—Lily, eleven years old.[7]

"I think Harry Potter is absolutely fine!...I like how they [Harry and his friends] can use witchcraft for fun/good purposes."

—Devon, eleven years old.[8]

"The book made me want to go to Hogwarts. Hogwarts is a school for teaching magic. I would like to learn magic, but I haven't gotten my invitation yet."

—posted on www.amazon.co.uk, age unknown.[9]

"I wish Hogwarts were real because then I could go and learn magic instead of quadratic equations."

—Mairead, thirteen years old.[10]

Mrs. Rowling herself confessed to *Newsweek*:

I get letters from children addressed to Professor Dumbledore, and it's not a joke, begging to be let into Hogwarts, and some of them are really sad. Because they want it to be true so badly they've convinced themselves it's true.[11]

"Letters from children...it's not a joke, begging to be let into Hogwarts"? Kids who "want it to be true so badly they've convinced themselves it's true"? Obviously, a *desire* for witchcraft—to be let into Hogwarts—is being awakened in the minds of young readers. "They *want* it to be true so badly they've convinced themselves it's true." I wonder why? By now, the answer should be clear: *the Potion* again. Because there's so much reality mingled with the fantasy, kids are not only confused, but they want to do it themselves. And based on the above quote, it seems Mrs. Rowling herself is naively mystified over the effect her own books are having upon her readers.

So what does a young person do who "wants it to be true so badly" but then realizes, "Oh well, Hogwarts is out...now what?" Allow me to offer this simple scenario illustrating how easy it is to transition from Step one to three.

Step 1: *Reading* Harry Potter

Step 2: *Wanting* the real thing

Step 3: *Involvement* in real witchcraft

Joe Teenager loves *Harry Potter and the Sorcerer's Stone, Harry Potter and the Chamber of Secrets, Harry Potter and the Prisoner of Azkaban, Harry Potter and the Goblet of Fire, Harry Potter and the Order of the Phoenix, Harry Potter and the Half-Blood Prince*—and hasn't missed a movie. As Joe is increasingly hooked by Rowling's storytelling abilities, and as his mind becomes saturated with the fantasy-mixed-with-reality world of his spellcasting hero, the idea of becoming a powerful wizard himself pops into his brain. *What an awesome thought!* Especially when compared to his miserably boring life in a fatherless home with an alcoholic mother and mean brother.

One dark night (after another bout with math and English), Joe quietly sits down before his refurbished Sony computer, boots up, logs onto the Net through an inexpensive dial-up connection, and types in, www.yahoo.com. In the blank field he quickly pecks "Harry Potter," then clicks "Find." As Yahoo's search engine instantaneously scours the vast world of cyber space, it quickly registers 4,240,000 (I just did it and that's the number it gave) *Potter*-related web sites to surf around in.

Of course, Joe finds Warner Brother's official site filled with fantastic images of Hogwarts and the magical world of the homely, dark-haired, orphaned wizard-boy with big spectacles (to whom he can relate). Yet that site doesn't satisfy an awakened desire within. Returning to Yahoo, he types in "Witch." This quickly registers 2,310,000 web site options. The first reads, "We are the right place for all your Witchcraft, Wiccan, Pagan, Occult, and ritual supplies...receive our free catalog." With a click he enters an online store with 4,000 occult products easily shipped UPS Ground Services and paid for by Visa, MasterCard, or Pay Pal.

Click...click...after a bit more surfing, Joe checks out www. walmart.com and discovers a whole bunch of real witchcraft books targeting his age group—like Silver Ravenwolf's *Teen Witch: Wicca for a New Generation* (Llewellyn, 2003), or Jennifer Hunter's *21st Century Wicca: A Young Witch's Guide to Living the Magical Life* (Citadel Press, 1997), or Teresa Moorey's *Spellbound: The Teenage Witch's Wiccan Handbook* (Ulysses Press, 2002). One reviewer of *Spellbound* commented:

> Written by an experienced witch, Spell Bound answers every question young readers face as they explore Wicca and the practice of witchcraft...The author shows how to find ones power and use it responsibly, how to develop ones intuitive senses and find a magical identity, and how to create positive spells and celebrate Wiccan festivals. Ultimately, Spell Bound helps teenagers strengthen their inner ability to guide their own lives. By discovering the mystical ways of witchcraft, teens can make magic a part of their everyday life.[12]

Sounds great! Joe thinks to himself. Click...click...still inside walmart.com, he decides to read more about *Teen Witch: Wicca for a New Generation* and then notices the publisher's name, "Llewellyn Publications." *Hey!* Joe remembers. *I saw that name in **Harry Potter and the Order of the Phoenix!** Dai Llewellyn Ward...that's where Mr. Weasley went after almost being obliterated by Voldemort!* Joe buys the book or, if he doesn't have a credit card, picks one up at a local Barnes & Noble down the block.

Teen Witch explains how simple, normal, and downright kosher it is for any teenager to begin practicing the Craft. It even teaches Joe how to draw his own "magic circle" in his bedroom, what witchy words to repeat, what tools or substances he needs to cast certain spells (like how to get better grades in school), and what follow-up books he can read to learn more.

Back to the Net. "Wicca"... "Witchcraft," he types. So many options! Soon Joe discovers many online "Steps to Becoming a Witch" courses claiming that Wicca is perfectly harmless (if used responsibly), that it can rev-up his boring life, can help him deal with his mom's drinking problem, teach him how to a cast spell on his nasty brother, or woo a girl he may like, *all through the power of magic.* Joe picks one, zips through it, and soon becomes an initiate, thus joining countless other curious teenagers recently intrigued by the idea of becoming powerful wizards-in-training, *just like their spellcasting hero, Harry Potter.*

Harry Potter and the Chamber of Secrets drops a definite seed into the minds of kids that such study courses exist (believe me, they do). One day Harry found himself alone inside the office of one of the workers at Hogwarts. Spotting an envelope on a desk, he curiously opened it and read this short advertisement:

KWIKSPELL: *A Correspondence Course in Beginner's Magic*

Feel out of step in the world of modern magic? Find yourself making excuses not to perform simple spells? Ever been taunted for your woeful wand work? There is an answer!

Kwikspell is an all-new, fail-safe, quick result, easy-learn course. Hundreds of witches and wizards have benefited from the Kwikspell method.[13]

Parents naively think, "It's just fiction!" but don't be fooled. *Similar* courses do exist, which can easily be found via any Dell, Compaq, E-Machine, or any other computer with a modem and Internet connection. Their numbers are growing rapidly in cyberspace, and lots of kids are letting their fingers do the walking on their keyboards to become Wiccan initiates. Not only that, but plenty of web sites are popping up where teenagers interested in Wicca can read messages from other teens, exchange email addresses, chat online, ask questions, swap spells, and even find information about establishing or joining local covens. And as I mentioned before, one web site comes from Llewellyn Publications—the same name used in *Harry Potter and the Order of the Phoenix!*[14]

Richard Abanes understands how easy it is to shift from *Harry Potter* to real sorcery:

> Ultimately, only a short distance needs to be covered in order to cross over from Harry's world into the realm of real occultism.[15]

No doubt. With the popularity of *Harry Potter* and today's exploding interest in witchcraft among teenagers, it should be overwhelmingly obvious to everyone that many *are* crossing over from Harry's world into the real thing. Now let's get down to details. *Why* is Wicca witchcraft so bad anyway? *Why* does the Bible forbid all involvement with the occult, teach that those who do such things are "an abomination to the Lord," and say practitioners are ignorantly rushing toward "the lake of fire"? Was the rebel angel correct when he implied through the snake that God was really a freedom restrictor, a selfish tyrant, a Being whose Word need not be obeyed? Is God a mammoth Muggle-in-the-Sky seeking to prevent us from learning the secrets of the universe and finding happiness?

Let's find out...

ENDNOTES

1. Lindy Beam, "Exploring Harry Potter's World," *Teachers in Focus*, December 1999, available online at www.focusonthefamily.org. Quoted by Abanes in *Harry Potter and the Bible*, p. 1.

2. Robert Night, quoted in Deidre Donahue, "Are Parents Pushing 'Potter' on the Young," *Tulsa World*, June 20, 2000; cf. *USA Today* article of the same title, available at www.northernlight.com.

3. See www.paganfed.demon.co.uk.

4. Reported in *This Is London*, in an article entitled, "Potter Fans Turning to Witchcraft," August 4, 2000, available at www.thisislondon. co.uk. Referenced in Abanes, *Harry Potter and the Bible*, p. 66.

5. Andy Norfolk, quoted in *This Is London*, Ibid.

6. Quoted by Abanes, *Harry Potter and the Bible*, p. 128. Letters to the Editor, "What Readers Think about 'Goblet,'" *San Francisco Chronicle*, July 26, 2000, available at http://sfgate.com.

7. Abanes, p. 128. Lily, "Reader Comments," http://hosted.ukoln. ac.uk/stories/gallery/reviews/rowling/rowling-stone.htm.

8. *Ibid*., p. 129. Devon, "Readers Comments," http:// yabooks.about.com/teens/yabooks/bl_potter2_more1.htm?terms= occultism+Potter.

9. *Ibid*., p. 129. Customer Reviews, statement online at amazon.com.uk.

10. *Ibid*., p. 129. Mairead, "Readers Comments," http://yabooks. about.com/teens/yabooks/bl_potter2_more7.htm.

11. Malcolm Jones, "The Return of Harry Potter!" *Newsweek* (Online), July 1, 2000, p. 4. Quoted by Abanes in *Harry Potter and the Bible*, p. 124.

12. See http://www.walmart.com/catalog/product.gsp? product_id= 1741619. Quoted "as is."

13. Rowling, *Chamber of Secrets*, p. 127.

14. See http://teen.llewellyn.com; Rowling, *Order of the Phoenix*, p. 487.

15. Abanes, *Harry Potter and the Bible*, p. 173.

CHAPTER 12

THE ANALYSIS:
What Is Wrong With Wicca?

We should educate people that "Witch" is not evil but
ancient and positive. The first time I called myself
a "Witch" was the most magical moment of my life.
—Margot Adler in *Drawing Down the Moon:*
Witches, Druids, Goddess-Worshippers,
and Other Pagans in America Today[1]

When most Christians think about witches, they often imagine weird people dressed in strange clothes, holding séances in dark rooms, worshiping satan, sacrificing animals, and drinking blood. While it's true that some occultists *do* practice these things, most modern Wiccans don't; they aren't nearly as nightmarish as many think.

Your neighbor or coworker might be a witch; or your boss. A friend of mine told me her aunt practices Wicca. "She's my favorite aunt," she confided, "though I disagree with her beliefs." Those embracing Wicca now include doctors, dentists, teachers, students, school administrators, CEOs, businessmen, police officers, mechanics, military chaplains, accountants, writers, athletes, government officials, celebrities, housewives—people from all walks of life.

Wiccan Scott Cunningham, in his *The Truth About Witchcraft*, confirms:

> It's practiced by 12-year-old girls and senior men and women. Professionals, laborers, lawyers, and salespersons, all kinds of different people, perform spells.[2]

In a similar work, *The Truth About Witchcraft Today*, the same author reveals how Wicca witchcraft is rapidly advancing around the world:

> As a religion, Wicca exists throughout Europe; in all fifty of the United States; in Central and South America; in Japan, and elsewhere.[3]

Mr. Cunningham is reporting facts here—Wicca is *global*, and is now being practiced by millions of people. As mentioned previously, as far as the United States goes, since the 1990s the Craft has entered mainstream society; and information, books, and articles about this growing movement can now be found all over the Internet and in most bookstores. Fritz Ridenour, in his book, *So What's the Difference? A Look at 20 Worldviews, Faiths and Religions and How They Compare with Christianity* (2001), candidly adds: "Wicca is now recognized in the United States as a legitimate religion, protected by law and given tax-exempt status."[4]

The U.S. Constitution guarantees religious freedom to all Americans, and this also applies to Wiccans. They have a legal right to be witches if they choose, as long as they operate according to the laws of the land. Beyond this—as we saw earlier—witchcraft is becoming highly profitable to publishers, television and film producers, bookstores, toy stores, and malls. Witchcraft sells—and moneymakers are thrilled to capitalize on the craze. Get used to it. Wicca's here to stay.

In my opinion, one factor contributing to Wicca's growth is the earnest efforts of modern practitioners to clarify to an inquiring public what Wicca really is, what it isn't, and how so many "Church" people are grossly misinformed. "Christians don't have their facts straight,"

Wiccans often say. And many times, they're right. This hurts Christianity and aids the Wiccan cause by giving witches a chance to show where Christians are wrong.

For example, Christians often assume Wiccans are out-and-out satan-lovers. They're not. Wiccans don't even believe lucifer exists. Best-selling author Silver Ravenwolf clarifies in her Author's Introduction to *Teen Witch: Wicca for a New Generation*:

> [Wiccans] don't believe in the Devil. The Devil belongs to the Christian religion, not to the Old Ways. Witches believe that if you give something evil a name, then you give it power, so they stay away from things that are evil, including the Christian devil.[5]

Seeking to enlighten inquiring searchers, Ravenwolf reports:

> Witchcraft or Wicca is *not* a cult. Witchcraft or Wicca is a *legitimate* religion. Our clergy can legally marry people. We also have christenings (Wiccanings or Sainings) for our babies, just like other religions. We do the sprinkle-water-thing, too. In 1994, at the World Parliament of Religions in Chicago, Illinois, Wicca or Witchcraft was acknowledged as a legitimate religion by the other religions of the world, including Catholics, Jews, Buddhists, and many Protestant Christians. Witches can legally have churches in this country.[6]

Wiccans are entering politics to represent their interests, counteract misinformation, and lessen hostility against practitioners. Mrs. Ravenwolf declares:

> We do have several organizations now operating within the community, including WADL (Witches Anti-Discrimination Lobby); WARD (Witches Against Religious Discrimination); WPLA (Witches League of Public Awareness); and several others.[7]

Many reading *Hour of the Witch* may be shocked by all this. You might be thinking to yourself, *I had no idea!* Yet these are facts. After researching and pondering these things, I have come to this conclusion:

Christians in general—in their attempt to deal with Wicca and even to reach out to witches with the Good News—should make every effort to represent Wiccan beliefs fairly, and even to speak respectfully to those who have chosen that path. After all, they're human beings like we are, and God loves them, too, right? Some may need to adjust to this idea. That's okay. *Adjust.*

As the *Harry Potter* books somewhat accurately portray, Church history *is* filled with cruel "Burning Times" (A.D. 1300s–1600s) and persecution against witches that shouldn't be justified by anyone who believes the New Testament. "Love your neighbor as yourself" (Matt. 22:39) is the teaching of Jesus Christ, and this applies to Muslims, Buddhists, Hindus, Protestants, Catholics, Jews, atheists, and followers of the Old Religion also. This means—according to the doctrine of Christ—that we should *love witches, too.* Have you adjusted yet?

What about Old Testament verses that say witches should be stoned? They're still there, but in those days death penalties were executed against idolaters, adulterers, blasphemers, and Sabbath breakers, too (see Deut. 5:6-11; Lev. 20:10; Lev. 24:16; Num. 15:32-36). That was when God directly ruled over Israel—which would be called a theocracy. But in New Testament times we're told to wait patiently for the Day of Judgment, to bless our enemies, and to reveal Jesus Christ's love to all (see Rom. 12:19-21; Heb. 10:30; Matt. 5:43-48; John 3:16; 1 John 4:7-11). Bottom line: There's no excuse for persecution against Arabs, Jews, African-Americans, or anyone else, including Wiccans.

So what exactly do Wiccans believe? And if they're wrong, *why* are they wrong?

Before finding out, first I'm going to let Silver Ravenwolf relay the circumstances behind her choice to switch from Christianity to the Craft. You read that right. She was a Christian before becoming a witch! As Silver describes her shift, this will help clarify Wiccan beliefs. "I was a young Baptist kid with two average American parents," she reflects. "From my very young years to age seventeen, we regularly

went to a little red brick Baptist church nestled in the center of town."
What happened? Here's her story:

> Neither of my parents were Bible-thumpers, but each held re-
> ligion sacred in their own way. When I turned thirteen, my
> cousin, Tess, gave me a pack of tarot cards...I looked up to
> Tess, seven years older than me, blond, blue-eyed, athletic,
> and incredibly smart, the blood of an artist coursing through
> her veins. Tess was everything I wasn't.

> One summer afternoon she came to visit me. We walked into
> the fields behind my house, just enjoying the warm sun and
> laziness of the day. After thirty years, I can't recall all of the
> conversation, but what I do remember changed my life forever.

> "What they tell you in church isn't the whole truth," Tess said
> quietly...

> "A long time ago," she said, as she stared up at the fleecy
> white cloud scuttling across the sky, "religion was different.
> Did you know, for instance, that everyone on the planet
> thought God was a woman?"

> My eyes popped out at that one. A woman? No one in the
> Baptist church had ever said anything about God being a
> woman. That was news.

> She nodded at my shocked expression. "And did you know
> that in the medieval times men were so afraid of women that
> the Christian men of the day killed two million people, most-
> ly women and children. The historians call that era The Burn-
> ing Times. The Christian men claimed the women were
> Witches...You can check it all out in the history books," she
> continued. "The real ones, I mean. Not the junk they spoon
> you in school. Go to the library. You'll see."

> "And the Witches..." I breathed.

> "Well, to begin with, they don't believe in the Devil. The
> Devil belongs to the Christian religion, not to the Old Ways.
> Witches believe that if you give an evil thing a name, then

you give it power, so they stay away from things that are evil, including the Christian Devil." I scrambled to catch up with her because she had picked up her pace.

"You mean witches aren't bad?"

"No. Some people want you to think that the Witches are bad, but they aren't. Real Witches don't believe in hurting people. In fact, they take an oath of service to help people the best way they can."

"Wow!" My mind reeled. "Why hadn't my parents told me the truth about the Witches?…what about all those movies that show Witches as demented, evil people? What about those?" I asked.

Tess laughed. "They're just movies, silly. Stories that need a plot. None of those people who wrote that junk really investigated anything. They want money and thrills. They aren't interested in the truth."

"The truth?" I echoed.

"The truth?" she said firmly. "Here…" she rummaged through her purse. "I brought something for you." She stopped walking and dug to the bottom of the leather bag. I liked that purse. Its leather fringes danced and spun as she moved the things around inside. Curious, I inched closer, trying to peer around her scrabbling hand. In a flourish she produced a pocket book, and handed it to me.

"*Diary of a Witch*," I read aloud, "by Sybil Leek. Who is she?"

"Read it and find out," said Tess with a mysterious look in her eye. She looked over her shoulder as if, way back at the house, someone would hear us. "Don't ask me how I know, but I'm supposed to give this book to *you*. That's why I came over here…"

In the coming years I would investigate all that Tess told me. I would have many good conversations with my father on

THE ANALYSIS: What Is Wrong With Wicca?

topics like reincarnation, God, magick, the divine female, and lots of other things. In the end, whether by accident or design, I would become one of the most well-known Wiccan authors of my time. Now don't that beat all? And all from the gift of one three-dollar paperback.[8]

That's how this young Baptist kid switched from Christianity to witchcraft. Silver's testimony also shows *the power of books*—"one three-dollar paperback"—to set one's life on a different course. Remember the Johnny's-reading-a-book argument in favor of *Harry Potter?* I wonder if Silver's church-going parents (if they're still alive), as they reflect on their daughter's decision to read *Diary of a Witch*, are thinking, "How wonderful! Our little girl read a book!" I doubt it.

Now Silver Ravenwolf writes her own books about witchcraft explaining the very things she first learned from her blond cousin, Tess. Within *Teen Witch* are two sub-sections entitled, "The Basic Theology of Wicca" and "The Principles of Wiccan Belief," where she clarifies what witches believe. Throughout her book she lists other beliefs as well. Here are some of the main ones:

Witchcraft is a nature-based, life-affirming religion that follows a moral code and seeks to build harmony among people, and empower the self and others...[9]

We commune with streams, sky, fire, trees, animals, and rocks, much like the indigenous ancestors of America. We see everything on our planet as a manifestation of the Divine...[10]

We acknowledge a depth of power far greater than is apparent to the average person. Because this power is far greater than ordinary, we sometimes call this force "supernatural," but we see this power as lying within that which is naturally potential to all...Everyone has these abilities, but most don't use them, and some people fear these powers. Witches, and other enlightened souls, strive to strengthen these natural gifts.[11]

There is no right way to practice the Craft.[12]

We do not accept the concept of "absolute evil," nor do we worship any entity known as "Satan" or "the Devil" as defined by Christian Tradition.[13]

Not bound by traditions from other times and cultures, we owe no allegiance to any person or power greater than the Divinity manifest through our own being.[14]

God is within us and around us, willing to help us if we only ask.[15]

Witches see God as both masculine and feminine, so we often call God the Lord and the Lady.[16]

No religion is wrong in the way they see God.[17]

One of the primary building blocks of the Wiccan faith includes belief in reincarnation. When Witches die, we believe that we go to a place called the Summerland. In this realm of joy and learning, we reunite with those we love and begin to reassess our life on earth. When we are ready, we return to the earthly plane to continue to work out our Karma.[18]

Witches draw power from several sources, including Spirit, the Elements, the Ancestors, and the Angels.[19]

The moral code Mrs. Ravenwolf refers to is "The Wiccan Rede" (summarized by two words: "Harm none") and "The Threefold Law of Return" (what you dish out will return triple). Concerning the Wiccan Rede, Scott Cunningham testifies:

> Folk magic, as we have seen, is governed by one basic dictum: Harm none. As a religion embracing magic, Wicca follows the same rule, though it is often worded differently: *"An it harm none, do what you will."*[20]

Basically this means, "Use magic; just don't hurt anyone." Obviously, not harming anyone is a great idea, and I'm sure many Wiccans seek to follow this, which is another reason why we should have Jesus Christ's love in our hearts as we think about—and even talk to—those who embrace the Wiccan way. But let's go beyond this rather simplistic and highly relative moral code—just don't hurt anyone—and explore Wicca's belief system; especially the "magic" part.

Throughout *Teen Witch*, Silver Ravenwolf makes it clear that most Wiccans believe:

God is a universal force of positive energy.

God is both male and female.

There is a Mother Goddess.

Planet Earth is Divine.

Nature is filled with energy and spirits.

Magic is a legitimate method of tapping into Nature's power.

Witches can communicate with the spirits of the dead.

Witches go to Summerland after death.

Reincarnation happens to everyone.

Divinity is within us all.

The Self is God.

Scott Cunningham agrees with Ravenwolf, conveniently summarizing Wiccan beliefs into five essentials:

1. Worship of the Goddess and God
2. Reverence for the Earth
3. Acceptance of magic
4. Acceptance of reincarnation
5. Lack of proselytizing activities[21]

Of interest to Christians—and to all who believe the Bible—Mr. Cunningham also clarifies:

There is no sin, certainly not original sin, in Wicca. There is no Heaven or hell. There are few rules save for that which also governs folk magic: Harm none.[22]

Because, as Ravenwolf stated, "there is no right way to practice the Craft," there's plenty of variety within Wiccan beliefs, traditions, and practices. Yet most witches should agree that the above statements—coming from practicing witches themselves—do fairly and accurately reflect the general belief system of modern Wicca. No sin, no Heaven, no hell, and definitely *no devil*—this is pretty standard. Now it's time to compare Wicca's major beliefs with the Bible. As we do, it should be quite clear—from a biblical perspective—exactly *what's wrong with Wicca.*

Nature Is Divine:

To most witches, nature isn't only a manifestation of God's power, but nature *is* God. Scott Cunningham says:

> There is power in the universe...The Earth, the solar system, the stars—all that is manifest—is a product of this power. This power is within all things. It is within humans, plants, stones, colors, shapes, and sounds.[23]

To Cunningham and other witches, a majestic tree, colorful flower, flowing stream, or crawling bug isn't only a manifestation of God, but these things *are* God. Divinity literally dwells inside of everything. And because the earth and universe is filled with many different life forms and objects, the flip-side of this God-in-everything idea is that there are really many different gods and deities.

Scott Cunningham comments:

> Religious magic is that which is performed in the name of, or with the assistance of, deities. It has been practiced by peoples all over the world, at all times in history. In earlier ages, deities of the fields, the mountains, springs and woods were invoked during magic. The Moon and Sun were thought of as deities (or representations of them), and were called upon during magic ritual. This was, perhaps, the purest form of magic.[24]

The twin belief-system that (1) nature is God, and (2) nature houses many gods, is called "pantheism." *The American Heritage Dictionary* of the English Language (Fourth Edition, 2000) defines pantheism as:

Noun:

1.　A doctrine identifying the Deity with the universe and its phenomenon.

2.　Belief in and worship of all gods.

But this is not what the Bible says. Scripture rejects the notion of little deities—some friendly and some cruel—floating around within rocks, wind, fire, trees, or frogs. In the Bible there's only one God, the Maker of Heaven and earth, and when we look at nature's beauties, we see His hand, *not Him.* The Creator is exalted above His creation and is distinctly separate from it.

The Lord told Jeremiah:

Thus you shall say to them: "The gods that have not made the heavens and the earth shall perish from the earth and from under these heavens" (Jeremiah 10:11).

In the Bible, all little gods and pagan deities—Zeus, Apollo, Ra, Diana, Athena, Baal, or Neptune—are false gods. They're illusions. They don't exist. And any attempt to worship nature itself or any of these so-called gods is actually a sin against the Great Creator who made everything.

Notice carefully:

[They] *exchanged the truth of God for the lie, and worshiped and served the creature rather than the Creator, who is blessed forever. Amen* (Romans 1:25).

Appreciating nature is good; we should respect and enjoy the beautiful things God has made. In fact, we all need to spend much more time away from cars, noise, cities, and smog. "Come to nature," whispers the Wiccan. In our highly urbanized, stressed-out world, this appeal rightly tugs on the heart—like an echo from Eden—contributing greatly to the pull of the Craft. We should realize that the problem with Wicca isn't nature itself or our legitimate need to soak up its calming influences. Rather, it's that witches have gone too far by worshiping "the creature *rather than the Creator*." Without realizing it, they've meandered off the true path and exchanged "the truth of God" for a "lie"—a bad transaction. They're honoring God's works above the Worker, His art above the Artist, His painting above the Painter, rocks above the Rock of Ages. What a tragedy! This is the first thing wrong with Wicca.

The Lord and the Lady:

Ravenwolf states:

Witches see God as both masculine and feminine, so we often call God the Lord and the Lady.[25]

Mr. Cunningham confirms:

Current Western religion, says the Wiccans, is out of balance. Deity is usually referred to as God, as opposed to Goddess...The Wiccans are different. They view nature as a manifestation of deity. Because of this, they believe that a male divinity revered without a female deity is, at best, only half correct. Both sexes exist in nature. If nature is a manifestation of divinity, then divinity also manifests itself in male and female forms. Hence, modern Wicca usually is centered around reverence of the Goddess and the God as aspects of the universal power. Both, not one, not the other.[26]

The notion of a heavenly mother appeals to many women and accounts somewhat for the Craft's recent growth among females (most witches are women). "Women especially are drawn to it because of its acceptance of the feminine aspect of Divinity—the Goddess."[27] "In the Goddess We Trust" could be Wicca's motto. Witches often say things like, "The goddess was worshiped around the world, until men took over. But it's still part of the Old Religion." As cousin Tess told young Ravenwolf:

"A long time ago," [Tess] said, as she stared up at the fleecy white cloud scuttling across the sky, "religion was different.

Did you know, for instance, that everyone on the planet
thought God was a woman?" My eyes popped out at that one.
A woman? No one at the Baptist church had ever said anything about God being a woman. This was news.[28]

When I first read this, I couldn't help thinking that young Silver
was more than a little bit gullible. The reason "no one at the Baptist
church had ever said anything about God being a woman" is simply because Baptists believe in the Bible, not witchcraft. In God's Word, there
is *no* "Lord *and* Lady"—no heavenly goddess or Mother Nature. During His earthly ministry, Jesus taught us to pray:

Our Father in heaven,
Hallowed be Your Name.
Your kingdom come,
Your will be done
On earth as it is in heaven
(Matthew 6:9-10).

This shouldn't discourage women in the least or leave them unful-
filled. In the Bible, God is presented as having both masculine traits
(wrath, judgment, and justice) and typically feminine qualities (kind-
ness and tenderness). He created both Adam and Eve. "Male and female He created them" (Gen. 1:27). The Lord also compares His caring
interest to that of a mother's love for her child (see Isa. 49:15). Thus,
both fatherly and motherly attributes dwell within His perfect heart.

Yet Wiccans have a point. Sometimes—as Scott Cunningham
says—"Western religion" *is* out of balance. All too often the sterner qualities of God's character are emphasized to the neglect of His tender, nur-
turing ones, creating a vacuum in human hearts—in both men and
women—which only furthers Wicca's appeal. To avoid this imbalance,
both justice and tender mercy should be taught and modeled by Christian
leaders, pastors, and parents. Nevertheless, the Bible doesn't call God
"Mother," but "Father"; He's "Abba" (meaning "daddy"), not mommy.

Tess' words to young Silver weren't altogether wrong either. The
worship of a heavenly goddess *is* an old practice, yet in Scripture it's

presented as bad, not good; as a *departure* from the right, not an original truth. Around 700 B.C., God pronounced judgments against Israel for mixing with His religion the almost universal pagan practice of adoring a cosmic female, saying:

> *Do you not see what they do in the cities of Judah and in the streets of Jerusalem? The children gather wood, the fathers kindle the fire, and the women knead dough,* **to make cakes for the queen of heaven;** *and they pour out drink offerings to other gods, that they may provoke Me to anger…Therefore thus says the Lord God: Behold, My anger and My fury will be poured out on this place—on man and on beast, on the trees of the field and on the fruit of the ground. And it will burn and not be quenched* (Jeremiah 7:17-20).

Here "the queen of heaven" is seen as a false god, an idea which provoked the true God to anger. This "queen" was not His lover, wife, sister, or twin, or any other legitimate manifestation of Deity. Instead, she was a *competing delusion*. The reason for God's hostility against goddess worship is because it seductively leads gullible human beings to adore, honor, and serve something that *doesn't exist* while neglecting the Great Creator—the Heavenly Father—the Source of life and blessing to both men and women.

When Silver Ravenwolf says Wiccans worship "the Lord and Lady," I'm sure she really believes some planetary female is smiling down on her. Yet according to the Bible, it isn't so. There's no heavenly woman, no female goddess, no mom in the sky. Rather, the belief is a "strong delusion" (2 Thess. 2:11), another thing wrong with Wicca.

Human Gods and Goddesses:

In a Beliefnet article entitled "The Witch Next Door," Kimberly Winston not only says that "Today's Wicca is goddess-based and earth-centered," but that it is devoted to "revering the divine in nature *and in human beings.*"[29] In *Teen Witch*, Silver Ravenwolf inserts a Wiccan poem which also teaches this core doctrine of the Craft: *Self is God.* Among other things, the poem says:

> I am the Mother of Nature,
> Who gives life to the Universe.
> From me all things proceed,
> And to me all things must return...
> And you who think to look for me,
> Know that your search and yearning shall never find me,
> Unless you know the mystery;
> That if you cannot find what you seek *within yourself,*
> Then you will never find it outside yourself.
> For behold, I have been with you from the beginning;
> And I am that which is attained
> At the end of desire.[30]

If we look discerningly, this poem communicates the same message spoken to Eve through the snake. Supposedly, the "Mother of Nature," from whom "all things proceed," clarifies the "mystery" that we must find *within ourselves* what we seek. The poem concludes, "I am that which is attained at the end of all desire."

In Heaven, lucifer *desired* to be God Himself (see Isa. 14:12-14) and that very impulse made him a devil. After convincing himself of this I-am-God delusion, somehow he persuaded sinless angels that they were little gods, too. Net result? They were all hurled down to Planet Earth. Then satan tempted Eve through the snake, promising:

*You will be **like** god, knowing good and evil* (Genesis 3:5).

This was "the lie" Paul identified in Romans 1:25, yet Eve bought it. She isn't the only one. Wiccans may not believe in the devil, yet the poem inside *Teen Witch* expresses satan's thoughts exactly. The idea of becoming a god or goddess is highly appealing to fallen human nature; fascinatingly, tantalizingly appealing. Witchcraft says to sinners, "We offer you Power—the strength of God and the 'goddess'—so why not join our enlightened society? Boys, you can be a powerful wizard like

Harry Potter. Girls, you can be like the *Charmed Ones*...a goddess!"
Such is the lure of the Craft.

Scott Cunningham reflects:

> It is the processes at work within the Wiccan—the blossom-
> ing of the consciousness of the Goddess and God within, the
> attunement with the seasons, the flow of Earth energy
> through the body—that constitutes true Wicca.[31]

According to the Bible, these very "processes at work within the
Wiccan—the blossoming of the consciousness of the Goddess and God
within," constitute Wicca's lie. This We-Are-God notion may seem like
a wondrous path to spiritual enlightenment, yet it's really a dark delusion. Ask Adam and Eve. After listening to the slithering serpent and
eating the forbidden fruit they realized not blissful God-consciousness,
but lonely nakedness. Trying to convince ourselves that we are really
little gods is about as profitable as a mouse imagining itself King of the
Jungle. It won't work. It's also a direct violation of the Ten Commandments, the first of which states, "You shall have no other gods *before
Me*" (Exod. 20:3). This was lucifer's root sin, and its promotion is
something else terribly wrong with Wicca.

Performing Magick:

Performing magick is the heart of witchcraft. It's what makes a
witch, a witch. It is also what makes Harry Potter, Harry Potter. Two
words should be distinguished:

1. "Magic," meaning sleight of hand; and

2. "Magick," which refers to what real witches do.

Real witches perform real "magick," not circus tricks; yet they
often use the other spelling—"magic"—to describe their activities.
Technically speaking, witches don't believe the source of their magick
is "supernatural," but natural. They see their power coming from
sources inherent within their own bodies, from nature, from God, the
"goddess," and from deities. Scott Cunningham states, "Magic is [only]
the movement of natural energies."[32] Silver Ravenwolf confirms:

We acknowledge a depth of power far greater than is apparent to the average person. Because this power is far greater than ordinary, we sometimes call this force supernatural, but we see this power as lying within that which is naturally potential to all...Everyone has these abilities, but most don't use them, and some people fear these powers. Witches, and other enlightened souls, strive to strengthen these natural gifts.[33]

Take note: This is the exact philosophy of the *Harry Potter* books—so don't tell me they don't teach any real witchcraft. Ravenwolf has just explained an essential, core doctrine of the Craft, and it's the same teaching found within J.K. Rowling's novels. Ravenwolf says, "We acknowledge a depth of power far greater than is apparent to the average person." Rowling calls all such average, non-magical souls, Muggles. Ravenwolf says, "...some people fear these powers," which is exactly what Professor Binns taught Harry Potter when he spoke about "an age when magic was feared by common people, and witches and wizards suffered much persecution."[34] Ravenwolf says, "Witches, and other enlightened souls" understand this truth—which is exactly what Rowling's books say about wizards. Thus we have a clear Ravenwolf/Rowling connection. And again, Ravenwolf's publisher is "Llewellyn," the same word Rowling used for a hospital ward dedicated to healing the sick!

Wiccans believe "a depth of power" resides within nature and can be tapped into, harnessed, controlled, and directed by those "enlightened" enough to know how. Scott Cunningham states (the bullets are his):

- There is a power in the universe.
- This power can be roused and concentrated.
- This power can be "programmed" with specific vibrations or energies to effect a specific result.
- This power can be moved and directed.
- This power, once moved, has an effect on its target.[35]

White witches (like Harry Potter and Albus Dumbledore) seek to direct this power toward good goals, whereas dark witches (like Voldemort) try to channel it toward evil ones. To accomplish whatever goals they may desire, real witches practice rituals, perform ceremonies, mediate, concentrate, call on spirits, and speak special phrases (like Harry Potter does to perform spells), for the purpose of accessing and directing this power to change things. This is what real witchcraft and *Harry Potter* is all about—the lure of the Craft.

Here's the problem. Lucifer's fatal mistake lay in his desire for power—God's Power—*separate from God Himself.* In the Bible, God doesn't tell us to harness, control, and direct His power to accomplish *our* purposes, but rather to *submit* to His power for the carrying out of *His* purposes. Jesus Christ clarified this issue forcibly in the Garden of Gethsemane the night before He died:

> *He went a little farther and fell on His face, and prayed, saying, "Oh My Father, if it is possible, let this cup pass from Me; nevertheless,* **not as I will, but as You will**" (Matthew 26:39).

The world's Redeemer humbled Himself and submitted to God's will, not His own, no matter what—even if it meant a horrifying, painful separation from His Father. He did it because "All we like sheep have gone astray; we have turned, every one, to his own way; and the Lord has laid on Him the iniquity of us all" (Isa. 53:6). In His complete humility and unreserved surrender to His Father's will, Jesus left "us an example, that [we] should follow His steps" (1 Pet. 2:21).

The Bible says:

> *God resists the proud,*
> *But gives grace to the humble.*
> *Therefore, submit yourselves to God.*
> *Resist the devil and he will flee from you* (James 4:6-7).

This reveals the great issue facing each of us—including Silver Ravenwolf, J.K. Rowling, every *Harry Potter* fan, and every witch.

Will we follow in the steps of lucifer, yield to pride, seek power, and attempt to become gods ourselves? Or will we forsake our sins, submit to God, and resist the devil in the Lord's strength? In light of James 4, it's clear we can either submit to God so that satan will flee from us, or we can reject our Creator, try to become midget gods ourselves, and have satan enter and work through us. Remember, the devil is an invisible "spirit who works in the sons of disobedience" (Eph. 2:2). Don't forget this.

Witchcraft seeks to access, direct, and control God's power—instead of humbly submitting to it—by performing occult techniques of magick. Here is one more thing wrong with Wicca.

Communication With Spirits:

Though not promoted so heavily to the public, embedded within Craft theology is the idea of communicating with, cooperating with, and receiving help from spirits. In fact, accessing the energy of spirits is one of the primary sources of witch power. Witches think the non-physical entities, deities, or "presences," they "connect" with through magick are spirits of nature, gods, the goddess, the deceased, or guardian angels.

Silver Ravenwolf candidly acknowledges:

Witches draw power from several sources, including Spirit, the Elements, the Ancestors, and the Angels.[36]

In *Teen Witch*, Ravenwolf describes a Wiccan ritual where four teenagers—George, Tom, Julia, and Annette—meet together to perform "magickal working." After creating a "magic circle," their invocations begin:

Julia, with her back to the center of the circle, faces outward, hands crossed over her chest, takes a deep breath, calms herself inside before she begins, saying,

**"Hail Spirits of the North, Powers of Earth,
Be with us here tonight."**[37]

Tom says, "Hail Spirits of the East, elements of Air;" Annette says, "Hail Spirits of the South, elements of fire;" George says, "Hail Spirits of the West, element of water...."[38] Then Annette steps forward, faces an altar, and says:

**"There is one power, which is God and the Goddess.
I hereby call upon the bountiful energies of the universe
to aid us in manifesting our petitions."[39]**

Here teenagers are being taught to call upon spirits, energies, god, and the goddess as they perform supposedly safe magic. After learning everything *Teen Witch* has to offer, an end-of-the-book advertisement for another Ravenwolf book called, *Angels: Companions in Magick*, further invites guys and gals to:

> Build an angelic altar... meet the archangels in medita-
> tion...contact your guardian angel...create angel sigils and
> talismans...work magick with the Angelic Rosary...talk to
> the deceased.[40]

From a biblical perspective, *this is the most frightening aspect of real witchcraft.* Because witches don't believe in a real devil, they're extremely vulnerable to unknowingly opening themselves up to being invaded by deadly satanic forces, which they assume are only spirits of nature, the gods, or the dead. In this area, witches aren't only dead wrong, but they can literally end up dead through the malicious power of evil angels who may even try to kill them (more on this later).

In our chapter called, "The Curse: What the Bible Says About Sorcery," we noted Deuteronomy 18:9-14 with its list of dangerous occult practices that God categorically told Israel to steer clear of. Immediately after warning against anyone "who practices witchcraft," His Word adds, "Or a medium, or a spiritist, or one who **calls up the dead**. For all who do these things are an abomination to the Lord" (Deut. 18:10-12).

"Mediums" and "spiritists" are those who channel thoughts from spirits just like Professor Trelawney did in *Harry Potter and the Prisoner of Azkaban* when an eerie voice muttered through her contorted lips, "IT WILL HAPPEN TONIGHT!" The phrase "one who calls up the dead" applies to any living human being who is trying to make contact with the supposed ghosts of deceased loved ones, or "ancestors."

In *Harry Potter and the Chamber of Secrets*, the spirit of a dead girl named Myrtle talked with Harry Potter:

> "I wish people would stop talking behind my back!" Said Myrtle, in a voice choked with tears. "I do have feelings, you know, even though *I am dead*."[41]

Such scenes may seem fun and friendly, but they reflect the deadly, diabolical doctrine of spiritualism—communication with the dead. In *Harry Potter and the Goblet of Fire*, another not-so-friendly scene emerges when Harry Potter and Lord Voldemort become locked in a scary, nightmarish duel in a cemetery. All seems lost until help arrives in the form of Voldemort's dead victims who begin materializing out of his wand. Suddenly:

> ...another head was emerging from the tip of Voldemort's wand...and Harry knew when he saw it who it would be...the woman was the one he'd thought of more than any other...The smoky shadow of a young woman with long hair fell to the ground...straightened up, and looked at him...and Harry, his arms shaking madly now, looked back into the ghostly face of his mother. "Your father's coming...," she said quietly, "Hold on for your father...it will be alright...hold on...." And he came...first his head, then his body...the smoky, shadowy form of James Potter blossomed from the end of Voldemort's wand.[42]

"Your father's coming"—*but he was dead!* No matter, through *emergency help from the spirits of his dead parents*, Rowling's hero again escapes Voldemort's deadly grasp. The subtle message to kids is: When you're in a pinch, the ghosts of deceased family members can help you. Yet God's Word plainly forbids all communication with "the dead" (Deut. 18:11-12). The Bible adds:

145

*Give no regard to mediums and **familiar spirits**; do not seek after them, to be defiled by them: I am the Lord your God* (Leviticus 19:31).

"Familiar spirits" look familiar. Taking physical form from be-yond the veil, these entities supposedly seek to comfort, guide, or help us when we need it—just like they helped Harry. But it's all a trick. All supposed "spirits of the dead" contacted or conjured through tech-niques of the "Craft" (or by any other means) are not the friendly ghosts of dead parents, your Uncle Bill, Aunt Sue, Elvis Presley, Mar-ilyn Monroe, Princess Diana, or any other deceased person. Neither are they spirits of wind, water, fire, or trees. According to God's Word, they're really "spirits of demons, performing signs, which go out to the kings of the earth and of the whole world, to gather them to the battle of the great day of God Almighty" (Rev. 16:14).

Whatever these sly entities claim, their goal is not our enlighten-ment, but our damnation. *This is why witchcraft is so dangerous and why God warns us so strongly against it.* Our Creator loves us and longs to protect us from being invaded by intelligent, tricky, *deadly fallen angels* who invisibly inhabit our atmosphere as they await the Day of Judgment. Communication with spirits is one of the biggest things wrong with Wicca.

After Death, Witches Go to Summerland:

In *Teen Witch*, Silver Ravenwolf posts this definition of the place where Wiccans supposedly go after death:

> Summerland *n.* A Wiccan version of Heaven, this is where our souls go after physical death to celebrate the afterlife and continue our spiritual education.[43]

> When it is our time, the Witches enter the Summerland. From the Spirit that moves and flows through the Lord and Lady, we continue to learn the mysticism of the universe so that we may return, life after life, to serve our brothers and sisters. In

each lifetime, Spirit guides us through learning experiences, preparing us along the way for our individual missions.[44]

All of this is reminiscent of the serpent's deceptive promise to Eve in Eden. If she ate the forbidden fruit, she would "not surely die" (as God plainly warned), but would enter a higher sphere of existence lasting forever.

> *Then the serpent said to the woman, "You shall not surely die. For God knows that in the day you eat of it your eyes will be opened, and you will be like God, knowing good and evil"* (Genesis 3:4-5).

In contrast to the serpent's first lie, the Bible says, "the wages of sin is death" (Rom. 6:23), not Summerland. Paul also wrote, "it is appointed for men to die once, but after this the judgment" (Heb. 9:27). Notice that men "die once"—so much for reincarnation. After the final judgment at the end of the world (see Rev. 20:11-13), "anyone not found written in the Book of Life was cast into the lake of fire" (Rev. 20:15). As we've already seen, many of those hurled into this fiery sea will be unrepentant sorcerers. As it is written:

> *But the cowardly, unbelieving* [those who don't believe the Bible], *abominable, murderers, sexually immoral,* **sorcerers** [those who practice witchcraft], *idolaters* [such as those who worship a non-existent female goddess], *and all liars* [those who believe and communicate the serpent's lies] *shall have their part in the lake which burns with fire and brimstone, which is the second death* (Revelation 21:8).

Solemn but true. Silver Ravenwolf should have been more careful on that lazy summer day when her blond cousin Tess first handed her a copy of *Diary of a Witch*. As "a young Baptist kid," she should have remembered Eve in Eden who, after tasting the forbidden fruit, offered some to Adam, who foolishly ate it. May God open the eyes of unsuspecting Wiccans before it's too late.

No Devil:

As we've already seen, Silver Ravenwolf confessed:

[Wiccans] don't believe in the Devil. The Devil belongs to the Christian religion, not to the Old Ways. Witches believe that if you give something evil a name, then you give it power, so they stay away from things that are evil, including the Christian devil.[45]

Scott Cunningham dittoes:

The power at work in folk magic is just that—power. It is neither positive nor negative, good nor evil.[46]

Mr. Cunningham also says that when witches point their wands toward the north, saying, "O Spirit of the North Stone, Ancient One of the Earth, I call you to attend this circle. Charge this by Your powers, Old Ones!" that this is "not a conjuration of a demon, but a summoning of natural energy."[47] His soothing assurance to those who might be wondering is, "No demonic power flows to help the spell-caster."[48]

The reason for his conviction is simple—he doesn't believe demons exist. How can "demonic power" flow through the spell-caster, when there's no devil? Thus witches call upon spirits, work magick, and open their minds to "the flow of Earth energy through the body"[49] without the slightest fear of luciferian influences.

Consider, for a moment, an African tribal boy wandering into the jungle at night unafraid of man-eating lions because he does not believe that they exist. Would he not be in serious danger despite his unbelief? In fact, the Bible compares satan to just that—a hungry lion crouched and ready to kill. Peter urges everyone to, "Be sober, be vigilant; because your adversary the devil walks about like a roaring lion, seeking whom he may devour. Resist him, steadfast in the faith…" (1 Pet. 5:8-9).

How can we resist an entity we don't believe in? We can't. The fatal flaw of Wicca is that it sees only one power in the universe, a neutral one, neither good nor evil, neither positive nor negative. To Wiccans, the central issue is how they use that power. Yet the Bible says this worldview is false, a myth, a deadly lie. In reality, there are *two* great powers working in the atmosphere and within human hearts. One is perfect and moral; the other superbly wicked. One is the superior power of God Almighty (which includes the Holy Spirit and the timely assistance of loyal angels); the other is the highly deceptive force of the rebel angel and sneaky demons.

Jesus Christ plainly taught this "two powers" message when He sent Paul to Jews and Gentiles:

> to open their eyes, in order to turn them from darkness to light, and from **the power of satan to God**, that they may receive forgiveness of sins and an inheritance among those who are sanctified by faith in Me (Acts 26:18).

"From the power of satan to God" says it all. Satan exists and has power. Yet God's power is far greater, and it is the work of true Christians to help Wiccans comprehend this. Witchcraft teaches no sin, no Heaven, no hell, and no devil. The Bible teaches sin, a real Heaven, a real hell, and a real devil who not only started this mess but who is now pleasantly charming humanity toward a fiery lake of burning brimstone—exactly where he's going (see Rev. 20:10,15).

"Satan...deceives the whole world" (Rev. 12:9). Tragically, this includes modern Wiccans and lots of Craft-exploring teenagers. They don't realize it and are as unconscious of this fearful reality as was Eve when she not only plucked the forbidden fruit herself but allowed the devil to work through her, leading Adam into sin. Dear friend, *demonic power does flow through witches*. That's why Paul lifted the curtain and called Elymas the sorcerer a "son of the devil" (Acts 13:8-10). In this light I plead: Don't resist God's counsel. Do what our Creator protectively commands us to do.

Avoid witchcraft entirely.

ENDNOTES

1. Margot Adler, *Drawing Down the Moon: Witches, Druids, Goddess-Worshippers, and Other Pagans in America Today* (Penguin Books, 1997), p. 461.

2. Scott Cunningham, *The Truth About Witchcraft* (St. Paul, MN: Llewellyn Publications, 2002), p. 6.

3. Scott Cunningham, *The Truth About Witchcraft Today* (St. Paul, MN: Llewellyn Publications, 2001), p. 4.

4. Fritz Ridenour, *So What's the Difference? A Look at 20 Worldviews, Faiths, and Religions and How They Compare With Christianity* (CA: Regal Books, 2001), p. 210. Reference made to Robinson, *Excerpts From a U.S. District Court Decision Recognizing Wicca as a Religion* found at the Wicca web site: www.religioustolerance.com.

5. Ravenwolf, *Teen Witch*, p. xx.

6. *Ibid.*, p. 15, italics added.

7. *Ibid.*, p. 235.

8. *Ibid.*, pp. xvi-xxi.

9. *Ibid.*, p. 4.

10. *Ibid.*

11. *Ibid.*, pp. 5-6.

12. *Ibid.*, p. 8.

13. *Ibid.*

14. *Ibid.*

15. *Ibid.*, p. 10.

16. *Ibid.*

17. *Ibid.*

18. *Ibid.*, p. 26.

19. *Ibid.*, p. 27.

20. Cunningham, *The Truth About Witchcraft*, p. 46.

21. Cunningham, *The Truth About Witchcraft Today*, p. 62.

22. Cunningham, *The Truth About Witchcraft*, p. 48.

23. Cunningham, *The Truth About Witchcraft*, p. 13.

24. Cunningham, *The Truth About Witchcraft*, pp. 19-20.

25. Ravenwolf, *Teen Witch*, p. 10.

26. Cunningham, *The Truth About Witchcraft*, p. 23.

27. Cunningham, *The Truth About Witchcraft Today*, p. 5.

28. Ravenwolf, *Teen Witch*, p. xviii.

29. Kimberly Winston, "The Witch Next Door," November 11, 2004. See http://www.beliefnet.com/story/155/story_15517.html. Italics added.

30. Ravenwolf, *Teen Witch*, p. 57.

31. Cunningham, *The Truth About Witchcraft Today*, p. 146.

32. Cunningham, *The Truth About Witchcraft Today*, p. 24.

33. Ravenwolf, *Teen Witch*, pp. 5-6.

34. Rowling, *Chamber of Secrets*, p. 77.

35. Cunningham, *The Truth About Witchcraft*, pp. 12-13.

36. Ravenwolf, *Teen Witch*, p. 27.

37. *Ibid.*, p. 81.

38. *Ibid.*, p. 82.

39. *Ibid.*, p. 84.

40. *Ibid.*, Advertisement at the back of the book.

41. Rowling, *Chamber of Secrets*, p. 157, italics added.

42. Rowling, *Goblet of Fire*, p. 667.

43. Ravenwolf, *Teen Witch*, p. 25.

44. *Ibid.*

45. *Ibid.*, p. xx.

46. Cunningham, *The Truth About Witchcraft*, p. 14.

47. Cunningham, *The Truth About Witchcraft Today*, p. 109.

48. Cunningham, *The Truth About Witchcraft Today*, p. 18.

49. Cunningham, *The Truth About Witchcraft Today*, p. 146.

CHAPTER 13

THE CHARACTERS:
Potter Morals

Some of the most famous books are the least worth reading.
—John Morely

Those exploring or practicing the Wiccan way are human beings like everyone else. Some have higher ethical standards than others. From a moral standpoint, what about J.K. Rowling's *Harry Potter* books? Do they really teach positive values to kids? "Definitely," *Potter* supporters positively affirm. "They promote friendship, loyalty, fair play, resisting evil, and a passion to survive against overwhelming odds. What's wrong with that?" Obviously, nothing's wrong with that. Let's take a closer look.

After Lord Voldemort murdered Harry's classmate, Cedric Diggory, Albus Dumbledore explained to his Hogwarts students:

> "Cedric was a person who exemplified many of the qualities that distinguish Hufflepuff House," Dumbledore continued. "He was a good and loyal friend, a hard worker, he valued fair play."[1]

> "I say to you all, once again—in the light of Voldemort's return, we are only as strong as we are united, as weak as we are divided. Lord Voldemort's gift for spreading discord and

enmity is very great. We can fight it only by showing an equally strong bond of friendship and trust."[2]

On the surface, Dumbledore's counsel sounds good, even biblical. The Scriptures also encourage unity, speak about houses not being divided, warn against sowing discord, and extol the importance of friendship and trust (see Eph. 4:3; Matt. 12:25; Prov. 6:19; 18:24). Thus *Harry Potter* apparently parallels the Holy Bible. But upon closer analysis, such similarities are exposed as entirely superficial. The contexts are vastly different. The Bible urges us to be united in our loyalty *to the Father, to His Son Jesus Christ, and to His Gospel*. Jesus said, "...that they also may be one in Us" (John 17:21). The Bible also tells us to resist satan, fallen angels, and sin—including the "sin of witchcraft" (1 Sam. 15:23).

The problem with *Harry Potter* is not its references to loyalty, friendship, fair play, and unity per se, but the story's underlying context of depicting such unity among witches and sorcerers—practitioners of mystical occult sciences that the Bible unequivocally condemns. Thus, while some ideas are good, the context is bad. The net result is that young readers are in danger of being subtly influenced toward seeing nothing wrong with witchcraft itself, or unity among witches.

Beyond contextual concerns, a closer look at the morals of even the "good" characters within *Harry Potter* leaves much to be desired. By today's standards, they don't seem too bad, and even appear virtuous. Yet as we're about to see, such virtue is shallow. When compared to the high standards of the Bible—standards all human beings should live by—the entire lot, including Harry, Ron, Hermione, the Weasleys, Hagrid, Sirius, and even Albus Dumbledore leave a trail of filth and moral stench unworthy of children's literature.

Let's start with **constantly breaking rules**. Is this a virtue? Take a look:

Harry felt he was pushing his luck, breaking another school rule today.[3]

Hermione had become a bit more relaxed about breaking rules.[4]

"There might be a way," said Hermione slowly, dropping her voice still further... "Of course, it would be difficult. And dangerous, very dangerous. We'd be breaking about fifty school rules, I expect—."[5]

"I never thought I'd see the day when you'd [Hermione] be persuading us to break rules," said Ron. "All right, we'll do it."[6]

After Professor Snape lamented how "Potter has been crossing lines ever since he first arrived at this school," Hagrid, Harry, Ron, and Hermione smugly reacted:

"Said that, did he?" said Hagrid, while Ron and Hermione laughed. "Well, yeh might've bent a few rules, Harry, bu' yeh're all righ' really, aren' you?"

"Cheers, Hagrid," said Harry grinning.[7]

Professor Snape moaned again:

"To me, Potter, you are nothing but a nasty little boy who considers rules beneath him."[8]

Late one night:

Harry planned his excursion carefully, because he had been caught out of bed and out-of-bounds by Filch the caretaker in the middle of the night once before, and had no desire to repeat the experience. The Invisibility Cloak would, of course, be essential, and as an added precaution, Harry thought he would take the Marauder's Map, which, next to the cloak, was the most useful aid to rule-breaking Harry owned.[9]

The evidence is clear: Harry Potter breaks rules, and more rules, and even has a Marauder's Map—"the most useful aid to rule-breaking Harry owned." After Harry and Ron broke a bunch of rules, but acted heroically, Dumbledore reflected:

"I seem to remember telling you both that I would have to expel you if you broke any more school rules," said Dumbledore.

Ron opened his mouth in horror. "Which goes to show that the best of us sometimes eat our words," Dumbledore went on, smiling. "You will both receive Special Awards for Services to the School and—let me see—yes, I think two hundred points apiece for Gryffindor."[10]

Thus, in spite of Harry Potter and Ron Weasley's rule breaking, a smiling Dumbledore finally honors them with Special Awards. Is this a good lesson for our kids? What parent doesn't struggle with teaching children the importance of obeying rules at home and at school? Will Harry Potter's example aid their cause? Hardly. The Bible even says one sign of "the last days" is that children will become increasingly "disobedient to parents" (2 Tim. 3:1-2), which would naturally spill over toward teachers, too. By rewarding rule-breakers, the *Harry Potter* books contribute to this end-time trend predicted to occur before the return of Jesus Christ.

The *Potter* books **don't teach respect for parents**, either. During one scene in *Harry Potter and the Goblet of Fire*, Harry's best friend Ron reacts against his own mother:

"Mum, shut up!" Ron yelled. "It's okay."[11]

Is shouting "shut up!" to your mother okay? Not according to my Bible. The Fifth Commandment speaks plainly to children, saying:

Honor your father and your mother, that your days may be long upon the land which the Lord your God is giving you (Exodus 20:12).

King Solomon warned:

The eye that mocks his father, and scorns obedience to his mother, the ravens of the valley will pick it out, and the young eagles will eat it (Proverbs 30:17).

Concerning general obedience to those in authority, the Book of Hebrews says:

Obey *those who rule over you, and be submissive, for they watch out for your souls, as those who must give account...* (Hebrews 13:17).

The undeniable truth is that Harry Potter and his friends are willful, persistent, almost constant breakers of school rules, and Mrs. Rowling herself apparently has a naughty taste for such disobedience. Parents, this is *not* a good sign. Don't be fooled. End-time kids should be taught to *obey* parents and teachers, and they should be reading books that promote this virtue instead of undermining it. Who was the first one to break God's Law in Heaven, anyway? You should know by now. Strike one for *Potter* morals. And these books are being encouraged in the United States public school system? Go figure.

One summer evening Harry Potter and his Muggle cousin Dudley Dursley just happened to cross paths outside their home on 14 Privet Drive. Granted, Dudley is no saint, but neither is Harry. Dudley had beaten up a boy and was defending his actions, when Harry jabbed:

> "Yeah? Did he say you look like a pig that's been taught to walk on its hind legs? Cause that's not cheek, Dud, that's true..." A muscle was twitching in Dudley's jaw. It gave Harry enormous satisfaction to know how furious he was making Dudley; he felt he was siphoning off his own frustration into his cousin, the only outlet he had.[12]

Harry not only called his cousin "a pig that's been taught to walk on its hind legs," but found "enormous satisfaction" making him mad. *But Dudley's really bad!* some might be thinking. No doubt. But does this justify such disgusting words from the lips of Rowling's superhero? In stark contrast, Jesus Christ taught:

> *But I say to you, love your enemies, bless those who curse you, do good to those who hate you, and pray for those who spitefully use you and persecute you, that you may be the sons of your Father in Heaven...* (Matthew 5:44-45).

Jesus presents quite a different lesson for children from what is being taught (and modeled) in the *Harry Potter* books. It wouldn't be so bad if Harry later felt sorry for his actions, but he doesn't. Instead, his actions are excused because "he was siphoning off his own frustration into his cousin, the only outlet he had." This is typical in the *Potter* books—an excuse is given. It's the same with Harry's rule breaking— it was for a good cause. *This is Harry Potter.*

Over and over again, Harry does *bad* things for "good" reasons. It seems Rowling herself doesn't care much for rules or nice language. Honestly, calling one's relative "a pig that's been taught to walk on its hind legs" is inexcusable, no matter what they do. In front of His murderers, Jesus Christ prayed, "Father, forgive them, for they do not know what they do" (Luke 23:34). Our Lord has left "us an example, that you should follow *His steps*" (1 Pet. 2:21). His pure steps lead far away from Harry Potter's slimy course of action.

Below we see another volatile scene in Harry's tumultuous life. This time Rowling's hero is in his dorm room when a classmate sincerely questions him about what really happened the night Voldemort murdered Cedric Diggory:

> He [Harry] got into bed and made to pull the hangings closed around him, but before he could do so, Seamus said, "Look…what did happen that night when…you know, when…with Cedric Diggory and all?" Seamus sounded nervous and eager at the same time. Dean, who had been bending over a trunk, trying to retrieve a slipper, went oddly still and Harry knew he was listening hard.
>
> "What are you asking me for," Harry retorted. "Just read the *Daily Prophet* like your mother, why don't you? That'll tell you all you need to know."
>
> "Don't you have a go at my mother," snapped Seamus.
>
> "I'll have a go at anyone who calls me a liar," said Harry.
>
> "Don't talk to me like that!"
>
> "I'll talk to you how I want," said Harry, his temper rising so fast he snatched his wand back from his bedside table. "If you've got a problem sharing a dormitory with me, go and ask McGonagall if you can be moved, stop your mummy worrying—"

"Leave my mother out of this, Potter!"[13]

Here Harry Potter attacked Seamus' mother, even though his fellow-student was only seeking a real answer to an honest question, not a fight. Oh yea, I forgot; Harry had an excuse—Seamus' mother believed some lies in the *Daily Prophet* (a witch newspaper) that made Harry look bad. Does this justify an unprovoked outburst of rage against a class-mate's mother? Parents, if you want your kids reading this stuff, that's up to you. I don't.

Harry Potter's diatribe against Seamus and his mother is not the only scene where angry outbursts flow from the wand-flicking wizard boy (we just saw how Harry taunted Dudley). Harry often has **temper tantrums**:

[Harry's] temper, always so close to the surface these days, was rising again.[14]

"Hermione says she thinks it would be nice if you stopped taking out your temper on us," said Ron.[15]

Amazingly, the same Bible verse that lists "sorcery" as one of "the works of the flesh" also warns that "outbursts of wrath" can close Heaven's doors against us (see Gal. 5:20-21). In contrast, we should learn "self-control," a fruit of the Holy Spirit (see Gal. 5:22-23).

Next "virtue": **Alcohol drinking**. Alcoholism is a devastating curse facing many societies. I still remember during one of my trips to Russia listening to the eerie songs of winos below our hotel window at 3:00 a.m. In the morning we saw them sleeping in bushes near side-walks, often in their own vomit. Not a pretty sight.

In the *Potter* books, Harry, Ron, Hermione, Sirius (Harry's god-father), Hagrid, and even Albus Dumbledore all drink alcohol. Even underage drinking occurs (to date, Harry is a 15-year-old). Such drink-ing is not presented as a moral slip, but as a cool practice. Another good example for our youth?

Sirius was hurrying toward them all, looking anxious. He was unshaven and still in his day clothes; there was also a slightly Mundungus-like whiff of stale drink about him.[16]

Near the end of book three, Albus Dumbledore pleasantly requested: "Hagrid, I could do with a cup of tea. Or a large brandy."[17] During one school trip to Hogsmeade (a nearby wizard village), Harry and his underage buddies gathered for a secret meeting inside a local pub:

> "You know what?" Ron murmured, looking over at the bar with enthusiasm. "We could order anything we liked in here. I bet that bloke would sell us anything, he wouldn't care. I've always wanted to try firewhisky—"...

> "So who did you say is supposed to be meeting us?" Harry asked, wrenching open the rusty top of his butter beer and taking a swig.[18]

On another occasion Harry and his friends sat at Sirius' house:

> "That's right," said Sirius encouragingly, "come on...let's all have a drink while we're waiting, *Accio Butterbeer!*" He raised his wand as he spoke and half a dozen bottles came flying toward them out of the pantry, skidding along the table, scattering the debris of Sirius's meal, and stopped nearly in front of the six of them. They all drank, and for a while the only sounds were those of the crackling of the kitchen fire and the soft thud of their bottles on the table.[19]

Here are a few more examples proving that the *Harry Potter* books often score low on the morality test (remember, we're talking about children's literature):

Smoking:

> Professor Grubbly-Plank [a Hogwarts Professor] appeared at Professor McGonagall's shoulder, smoking a pipe and holding a copy of the *Daily Prophet*.[20]

Lying:

Harry lied brutally.[21]

Harry lied quickly.[22]

Harry lied.[23]

Harry lied.[24]

Many more examples of Harry's lying could be listed. How strongly does the Bible oppose lying? Read Revelation 21:8. "All liars" who don't repent will end up in "the lake which burns with fire and brimstone, which is the second death." If Harry was a real person, he'd be in big trouble on Judgment Day—and no "marauder's map" or "invisibility cloak" could get him out of it.

Hating a teacher:

Harry looked back at Snape, hating him…[25]

Contemplating revenge:

[Harry] fell asleep contemplating hideous revenges and arose from bed three hours later feeling distinctly unrested.[26]

Swearing:

"Oh damn," whispered Ginny, jumping to her feet. "I forgot—"[27]

Mr. Weasley cursed furiously…[28]

"[Bill Weasley:] No one at the bank gives a damn how I dress."[29]

Gambling (and hiding the practice from a parent):

"*Don't* tell your mother you've been gambling," Mr. Weasley implored Fred and George as they all made their way slowly down the purple-carpeted stairs. "Don't worry Dad," said Fred gleefully, "we've got big plans for this money. We don't want it confiscated."[30]

Crude language:

"[Harry:] Yea, give Ron a good kick up the—"[31]

Ron told Malfoy to do something that Harry knew he would never have dared say in front of Mrs. Weasley.[32]

These are just a few examples of *rule breaking, temper tantrums, lying, swearing, smoking, drinking, contemplating revenge, cursing, gambling,* and *crude language* among young Harry, his teenage friends, and even Hogwarts teachers. Some have countered, "Yes, but people sin in the Bible!" True—but there's one major difference. In Scripture, whenever God's heroes (Abraham, Moses, David, Peter, etc.) commit sins or moral lapses, those acts are seen as just that—*sins* to be repented of. No excuses are offered. Not so in *Harry Potter*. In Rowling's books, excuses constantly justify bad behavior, and even obviously wrong actions—like lying and rule breaking—seem virtuous. *Virtuous* may not be the right word. *Cool* fits better.

In *Harry Potter and the Goblet of Fire*, Harry is introduced to his best friend Ron Weasley's older brother, Bill, whom he had never met.

Bill was—there was no other word for it—*cool*. He was tall, with long hair that he had tied back in a ponytail. He was wearing an earring with what looked like a fang dangling from it. Bill's clothes would not have looked out of place at a rock concert, except that Harry recognized his boots to be made, not of leather, but of dragon hide.[33]

Parents, do you want your son dressed like this? Like a rock star with a fang earring? Rowling presents Bill Weasley as *cool*—the stellar virtue among many teens. This reminds me of a TV commercial I saw where a man said to a smart-alecky teenage gal, "The problem with your generation is you don't have any values!" "Values?" the girl shot back. "Hey, this top cost less than $15. That's value!" Then a group of provocatively dressed guys and girls swayed back and forth to the beat of rock music while promoting the great deals of a clothing store.

Too often that commercial typifies the values of this generation. Not real moral values—like obedience, respect for authority, truth-telling, honesty, pure words, self-control, avoiding alcohol and tobacco, and clean living—but the value of being cool, just like Bill Weasley, *and especially, Harry Potter.* That so many parents and teachers can extol the "virtues" of *Potter* is shocking. It's either symptomatic that they have never really read those books, or that they haven't read the Bible; and if they have read the Bible, that they've failed miserably to understand its uncompromising statements about purity, humility, truthfulness, respect, and righteous living—lessons entirely absent from Rowling's supposedly "moral" productions. On the other hand, it could simply be symptomatic of the low state of society's morals in general which, according to Second Timothy 3:1-5, is a prophetic sign of "the last days."

Richard Abanes discerned clearly:

> Rowling's fantasy presents a morally confusing world where good characters (e.g., Harry, Ron, Hermione, Lupin, etc.) consistently resort to unethical behavior (e.g., lying, cheating, stealing, deception) to further their own goals that are supposedly "good."[34]

Harry Potter perfectly reflects today's "if it feels good do it" philosophy. This is Wicca witchcraft's idea also. Silver Ravenwolf says, "There is no one right way to practice the Craft. The religion is what you make of it."[35] Again Ravenwolf reports: "We owe no allegiance to any person or power greater than the Divinity manifest through our own being."[36] In other words, "Don't tell us what to do. We do what we want. We're gods!" This is how Harry Potter acts. One 11-year-old girl told Richard Abanes, "I like Harry because he can do whatever he wants to do."[37] Witchcraft inserts this mildly restraining dictum, "Harm none"; but who defines "harm" anyway? Wicca's answer is: *You do!*

In short, Rowling's moral universe is a topsy-turvy world with no firm rules of right and wrong or any godly principles by which to determine the truly good from the truly evil.[38]

One key difference between *Harry Potter*, Wicca witchcraft, and the Bible is that the Scriptures *do* have "firm rules of right and wrong." Moses didn't come down from Mount Sinai with ten suggestions, but with "Ten Commandments" (Deut. 4:13). The Bible says that having other gods, dishonoring parents, lying, and practicing witchcraft are *sins against God*. It even says that "those who practice such things are deserving of death" (see Exod. 20:3-17; 1 Sam. 15:23; 1 John 3:4; Rom. 1:32). These things are sins because they go against God's nature—against His character of love, truthfulness, integrity, and unselfishness. They have no permanent place in His universe. God painfully tolerates them now, but a Day is coming when "He shall judge the world with righteousness, *and the peoples with His truth*" (Ps. 96:13). "God will bring every work into judgment, including every secret thing, whether it is good or evil" (Eccles. 12:14). No spell can offer escape. Our only hope is the "Man With Scars" (more on this soon).

Here's one final section from *Harry Potter and the Order of the Phoenix*:

> At half-past seven Harry, Ron, and Hermione left the Gryffindor room, Harry clutching a certain piece of aged parchment in his hand. Fifth years were allowed to be out in the corridors until nine o'clock, but all three of them kept looking around nervously as they made their way up to the seventh floor. "Hold it," said Harry warningly; unfolding the piece of parchment at the top of the last staircase, tapping it with his wand, and muttering, "*I solemnly swear that I am up to no good.*" A map of Hogwarts appeared upon the blank surface of the parchment. Tiny black moving dots, labeled with names, showed where various people were.[39]

Here, during one of his many rule-breaking trips around Hogwarts, Harry Potter, the hero-wizard, taps his wand on a parchment, saying, "I solemnly swear I am up to no good." At the conclusion of film three, *Harry Potter and the Prisoner of Azkaban*, that single sentence pops onto the screen as the last thing kids see before the lights go on. May our mental lights go on as we contemplate these sober words of Jesus Christ:

> *But I say to you, do not swear at all: neither by heaven, for it is God's throne; nor by earth, for it is His footstool; nor by Jerusalem, for it is the city of the great King. Nor shall you swear by your head, because you cannot make one hair white or black. But let your "Yes" be "Yes," and your "No," "No."* ***For whatever is more than these is from the evil one*** (Matthew 5:34-37).

"Do not swear at all," taught Jesus. He also said that anything other than absolute truth "comes from the evil one." In the penetrating light of His purity and godly instruction, what do you think Jesus Christ would say about movies and books for children that make witchcraft seem cool and whose main character casts spells, lies, curses, drinks, has temper tantrums, breaks rules, and "solemnly swears" he is up to no good?

There's no need to guess. The Master has given us His answer: "For whatever is more than these *is from the evil one*" (Matt. 5:37).

If you are a follower of Jesus Christ, my simple advice to you and your kids is:

Avoid Harry Potter.

ENDNOTES

1. Rowling, *Goblet of Fire*, pp. 721-722.
2. Rowling, *Goblet of Fire*, p. 723.
3. Rowling, *Sorcerer's Stone*, p. 155.
4. Rowling, *Sorcerer's Stone*, p. 181.
5. Rowling, *Chamber of Secrets*, p. 159.
6. Rowling, *Chamber of Secrets*, p. 166.
7. Rowling, *Goblet of Fire*, p. 391.

8. Rowling, *Goblet of Fire*, p. 516.

9. Rowling, *Goblet of Fire*, p. 458.

10. Rowling, *Chamber of Secrets*, p. 331.

11. Rowling, *Goblet of Fire*, p. 712.

12. Rowling, *Order of the Phoenix*, p. 13.

13. Rowling, *Order of the Phoenix*, p. 218.

14. Rowling, *Order of the Phoenix*, p. 341.

15. Rowling, *Order of the Phoenix*, p. 237.

16. Rowling, *Order of the Phoenix*, p. 475.

17. Rowling, *Prisoner of Azkaban*, p. 402.

18. Rowling, *Order of the Phoenix*, p. 337.

19. Rowling, *Order of the Phoenix*, p. 477.

20. Rowling, *Order of the Phoenix*, p. 358.

21. Rowling, *Order of the Phoenix*, p. 682.

22. Rowling, *Chamber of Secrets*, p. 128.

23. Rowling, *Goblet of Fire*, p. 443.

24. Rowling, *Goblet of Fire*, p. 557.

25. Rowling, *Order of the Phoenix*, p. 591.

26. Rowling, *Order of the Phoenix*, p. 724.

27. Rowling, *Order of the Phoenix*, p. 655.

28. Rowling, *Order of the Phoenix*, p. 134.

29. Rowling, *Goblet of Fire*, p. 62.

30. Rowling, *Goblet of Fire*, p. 117.

31. Rowling, *Goblet of Fire*, p. 290.

32. Rowling, *Goblet of Fire*, p. 121.

33. Rowling, *Goblet of Fire*, p. 52.

34. Abanes, *Harry Potter and the Bible*, p. 254.

35. Ravenwolf, *Teen Witch*, p. 8.

36. *Ibid.*

37. Abanes, *Harry Potter and the Bible*, p. 38.

38. *Ibid.*, pp. 244-245.

39. Rowling, *Order of the Phoenix*, pp. 388, 390, italics added.

CHAPTER 14

THE BATTLE:

Prophecies in Conflict

I am God, and there is none like Me,
Declaring the end from the beginning,
And from ancient times things that are not yet done,
Saying, "My counsel shall stand,
And I will do all My pleasure."

(Isaiah 46:9-10)

eter wrote, "We have also a more sure word of prophecy" (2 Pet. 1:19 KJV). Biblical prophecy is more reliable than the ground we walk on. It reveals the rise and fall of nations, predicts future events, exposes satan's plans, and assures us that God's kingdom of love will someday be established in radiant glory. The Lord's prophecies are "more sure" than anything this world has to offer.

Peter also warned, "But there were also false prophets among the people, even as there will be false teachers among you" (2 Pet. 2:1). Thus we should be on guard against the subtle delusions of "false prophets" and "false teachers." Although the *Harry Potter* books don't contain any literal prophecies of the future, they do post one major prediction coming from a source other than God. As we might imagine, it is communicated through a witch.

Near the end of book five, *Harry Potter and the Order of the Phoenix*, Albus Dumbledore characteristically reflects on the school year and gives Harry Potter some concluding fatherly advice. Yet this time his end-of-term counsel concerns a mystical "prophecy" that was uttered before Harry's birth and which readers discover forms a key component in the entire drama between Harry Potter and the Dark Lord. Here's the entire context. Dumbledore explained to Harry:

> "Voldemort tried to kill you when you were a child because of a prophecy made shortly before your birth. He knew the prophecy had been made, though he did not know its full contents. He set out to kill you when you were still a baby, believing he was fulfilling the terms of the prophecy. He discovered, to his cost, that he was mistaken, when the curse intended to kill you backfired. And so, since his return to his body, and particularly since your extraordinary escape from him last year, he has been determined to hear that prophecy in its entirety. This is the weapon he has been seeking so assiduously since his return: the knowledge of how to destroy you…"

> "Who heard it [the prophecy]?" asked Harry, though he thought he knew the answer already.

> "I did," said Dumbledore. "On a cold, wet night sixteen years ago, in a room above the bar at the Hog's Head Inn. I had gone there to see an applicant for the post of Divination teacher, though it was against my inclination to allow the subject of Divination to continue at all. The applicant [Sibyll Trelawney], however, was the great-great-granddaughter of a famous, very gifted Seer, and I thought it common politeness to meet her. I was disappointed. It seemed to me that she had not a trace of the gift herself. I told her, courteously I hope, that I did not think she would be suitable for the post. I turned to leave."[1]

Then it happened. Before Dumbledore left the room, the woman he had just interviewed for a position at Hogwarts suddenly lost consciousness and unexpectedly became a medium for someone else's mind. Dumbledore continued:

> "But when Sibyll Trelawney spoke, it was not in her usual ethereal, mystic voice, but in the harsh, hoarse tones Harry had heard her use once before.
>
> 'THE ONE WITH THE POWER TO VANQUISH THE DARK LORD APPROACHES...BORN TO THOSE WHO HAVE THRICE DENIED HIM, BORN AS THE SEVENTH MONTH DIES...AND THE DARK LORD WILL MARK HIM AS HIS EQUAL, BUT HE WILL HAVE POWER THE DARK LORD KNOWS NOT...AND EITHER MUST DIE AT THE HAND OF THE OTHER FOR NEITHER CAN LIVE WHILE THE OTHER SURVIVES...THE ONE WITH THE POWER TO VANQUISH THE DARK LORD WILL BE BORN AS THE SEVENTH MONTH DIES...'"
>
> "Professor Dumbledore?" Harry said very quietly... "It...did that mean... What did that mean?"
>
> "It meant," said Dumbledore, "that the person who has the only chance of conquering Lord Voldemort for good was born at the end of July, nearly sixteen years ago. This boy would be born to parents who had already defied Voldemort three times."
>
> Harry felt as though something was closing in upon him. His breathing seemed difficult again. "It means—me?"
>
> Dumbledore surveyed him for a moment through his glasses... "I am afraid," said Dumbledore slowly, looking as though every word cost him great effort, "that there is no doubt that it is you...in marking you with that scar, he did not kill you, as he intended, but gave you powers, and a future, which have fitted you to escape him not once, but four times so far..."
>
> "There is a room in the Department of Mysteries...that is kept locked at all times. It contains a force that is at once

more wonderful and more terrible than death, than human intelligence; than forces of nature. It is also, perhaps, the most mysterious of the many subjects for study that reside there. It is the power held within that room that you possess in such quantities and which Voldemort has not at all. That power took you to save Sirius tonight. That power also saved you from possession by Voldemort, because he could not bear to reside in a body so full of the force he detests. In the end, it mattered not that you could not close your mind. It was your heart that saved you...."

Harry looked up at him and saw a tear trickling down Dumbledore's face into his long silver beard.[2]

Thus a prophecy was made through Sibyll Trelawney (who later became Harry Potter's Divination teacher) to Albus Dumbledore about a boy destined for birth in the seventh month who would have "power to vanquish the Dark Lord." Because Voldemort discovered part of the prophecy (not all of it), he tried to kill baby Harry (who was born in July, the seventh month), yet his efforts only further fulfilled the mysterious prediction. He ended up marking Harry as his equal (giving him that scar on his forehead), just like the prophecy said, and now both must wait and see who will destroy the other in the end.

Thus the entire *Harry Potter* saga is rooted in this strange "prophecy" given through Trelawney to Dumbledore in a room above the bar at the Hog's Head Inn. It's true, most of what comes through Sibyll Trelawney is quackery worth laughing at—but not this time. Twice in *Harry Potter* (at least through book five), Trelawney becomes an unconscious agency for true predictions. The first is in book three, *Harry Potter and the Prisoner of Azkaban,*[3] and the second was just quoted above. Both circumstances are similar: Professor Trelawney slips into an altered state of consciousness or trance, and an eerie, unknown, harsh voice speaks through her trembling lips.

In the real occult world this practice is called "channeling." Today, real mediums receive real messages from real spirits on the "other side." Although *Harry Potter* is mostly fiction, channeling surely isn't, and J.K. Rowling's *Order of the Phoenix* accurately depicts this practice and portrays it as resulting in a genuine prophecy which forms the background of her entire series. Like it or not, such a portrayal teaches this lesson to kids: Real spirits can give real prophecies through real mediums. Thus while *Harry Potter* doesn't contain any actual prophecies, it lends real credibility to real practices where real spirits give real prophecies in our real world to real people who are really being duped by a real devil. Peter not only warned about false prophets, but also said "there will be *false teachers* among you" (2 Pet. 2:1). What would Peter say about such "lessons" coming through the *Harry Potter* books?

In contrast to false prophecies that tricky fallen angels mutter through mediums, the Bible contains hundreds of true prophecies originating from God Almighty. One of the easiest to understand is located in the Book of Daniel, chapter 2. To this, we shall turn our attention.

Daniel was a Jewish captive from Jerusalem living in Babylon during the reign of King Nebuchadnezzar. The date was approximately 604 B.C. Because Daniel was intelligent, of royal lineage, and showed great promise to the Babylonian administration, he and his three friends were chosen as part of a group of wise-men-in-training being groomed to serve the king (see Dan. 1). Interestingly enough, most of Nebuchadnezzar's regular advisors were sorcerers.

One dark night, "Nebuchadnezzar had dreams; and his spirit was *so* troubled that his sleep left him" (Dan. 2:1). Waking up in cold sweat, sensing he had dreamed something terribly important, the king became frustrated as its foggy memory slipped beyond his awareness into realms unknown. *I must get that dream back!* he told himself. *But how? Who can help me? Ah, my trusted wise men!*

> Then the king gave the command to call the magicians, the astrologers, the sorcerers, and the Chaldeans to tell the king his dreams. So they came and stood before the king. And the king said to them, "I have had a dream, and my spirit is anxious to know the dream." Then the Chaldeans spoke to the

king in Aramaic, "O king, live forever! Tell your servants the dream, and we will give the interpretation." The king answered and said to the Chaldeans, "My decision is firm: if you do not make known the dream to me, and its interpretation, you shall be cut in pieces, and your houses shall be made an ash heap. However, if you tell the dream and its interpretation, you shall receive from me gifts, rewards, and great honor. Therefore tell me the dream and its interpretation" (Daniel 2:2-6).

King Nebuchadnezzar wanted his wise men to tell him *both* the dream and its meaning, thus proving their self-proclaimed ability to access secret knowledge; but they couldn't. The sorcerers were stumped!

They answered again and said, "Let the king tell his servants the dream, and we will give its interpretation." The king answered and said, "I know for certain that you would gain time, because you see that my decision is firm: if you do not make known the dream to me, there is only one decree for you! For you have agreed to speak lying and corrupt words before me till the time has changed. Therefore tell me the dream, and I shall know that you can give me its interpretation" (Daniel 2:7-9).

This was no fictitious encounter, and now the lives of these magicians were at stake. It was do or die, put up or shut up—or have their heads cut off. They couldn't perform. Their claim to hidden knowledge proved false. With knocking knees they responded again to the now-hot-under-the-collar king:

The Chaldeans answered the king, and said, "There is not a man on earth who can tell the king's matter; therefore no king, lord, or ruler has ever asked such things of any magician, astrologer, or Chaldean. It is a difficult thing that the king requests, and there is no other who can tell it to the king except the gods, whose dwelling is not with flesh" (Daniel 2:10-11).

In desperation, the magicians even blamed King Nebuchadnezzar for such an unreasonable request. Big mistake. He didn't appreciate such remarks.

> *For this reason the king was angry and very furious, and gave a command to destroy all the wise men of Babylon. So the decree went out, and they began killing the wise men and they sought Daniel and his companions, to kill them* (Daniel 2:12-13).

Executioners also showed up at Daniel's door because he and his friends were classified as among the king's wise men. Yet because Daniel had developed a friendship with the captain of the king's guard, he was allowed to seek a solution that might save his life.

> *Then with counsel and wisdom Daniel answered Arioch, the captain of the king's guard, who had gone out to kill the wise men of Babylon; he answered and said to Arioch the king's captain, "Why is the decree from the king so urgent?" Then Arioch made the decision known to Daniel. So Daniel went in and asked the king to give him time, that he might tell the king the interpretation. Then Daniel went to his house, and made the decision known to Hananiah, Mishael, and Azariah, his companions, that they might seek mercies from the God of heaven concerning this secret, so that Daniel and his companions might not perish with the rest of the wise men of Babylon* (Daniel 2:14-18).

The sorcerers had tried their crystal balls, tarot cards, tea leaves, astrological charts, and divination techniques; but nothing worked, and either satan wasn't able or wasn't willing to figure it out in their behalf. But Daniel had direct access to a superior Source of assistance unknown to the magicians. His trust was in the living God, the Maker of Heaven and earth. That night Daniel knelt quietly by his bed, said a prayer, and then drifted peacefully to sleep trusting in God's care. His faith was rewarded:

Then the secret was revealed to Daniel in a night vision. So Daniel blessed the God of heaven. Daniel answered and said: "Blessed be the name of God forever and ever, for wisdom and might are His. And He changes the times and the seasons; He removes kings and raises up kings; He gives wisdom to the wise and knowledge to those who have understanding. He reveals deep and secret things; He knows what is in the darkness, and light dwells with Him. I thank You and praise You, O God of my fathers; You have given me wisdom and might, and have now made known to me what we asked of You, for You have made known to us the king's demand" (Daniel 2:19-23).

Daniel knew the answer didn't come from self, nature, cauldrons, concentration, spirits, or any heavenly goddess—but from God alone. After gratefully thanking the Heavenly Revealer, he hastened back to the nervous sergeant.

Therefore Daniel went to Arioch, whom the king had appointed to destroy the wise men of Babylon. He went and said thus to him: "Do not destroy the wise men of Babylon; take me before the king, and I will tell the king the interpretation" (Daniel 2:24).

"Take me before the king" indeed! Arioch happily complied. So to the palace Daniel went, past meticulously manicured and blossoming gardens, bubbling waterfalls, through glistening corridors, and into the throne room of the greatest monarch on earth at the time. A lone Jew stood in front of the king.

Then Arioch quickly brought Daniel before the king, and said thus to him, "I have found a man of the captives of Judah, who will make known to the king the interpretation." The king answered and said to Daniel, whose name was Belteshazzar, "Are you able to make known to me the dream which I have seen, and its interpretation?" (Daniel 2:25-26)

174

The crucial moment had come. Well? Could Daniel discern *both* the dream and its meaning, or was his knowledge of hidden realities no better than the sorcerers? Nebuchadnezzar and Arioch waited breathlessly.

> *Daniel answered in the presence of the king, and said, "The secret which the king has demanded, the wise men, the astrologers, the magicians, and the soothsayers cannot declare to the king. But there is a God in Heaven who reveals secrets, and He has made known to King Nebuchadnezzar what will be in the latter days..."* (Daniel 2:27-28).

This passage is filled with heavenly light. Daniel reminded Nebuchadnezzar that all of his Babylonian wise men, magicians, astrologers, and soothsayers (occult practitioners) were clueless about the dream and its interpretation. They were about as profitable as paying $100,000 to a palm reader. Then Daniel divulged the golden key: "There is a God in heaven who reveals secrets." Ah yes; the Almighty has answers! The Lord gave the dream and explained its mysteries to his humble servant. Daniel took no credit for the insight; it wasn't because he had mastered any complex techniques or practices. He simply prayed, and God answered.

Again Daniel stressed that the answer didn't come because he was smart or special, but because he trusted God's mercy:

> *"But as for me, this secret has not been revealed to me because I have more wisdom than anyone living, but for our sakes who make known the interpretation to the king, and that you may know the thoughts of your heart"* (Daniel 2:30).

"More wisdom than anyone living" is what occultists claim. In fact, the word *occult* means "hidden knowledge." Occult practitioners think they understand hidden knowledge, while those who don't are ignorant Muggles. Yet Daniel 2 reveals that the supposed wisdom of sorcerers is foolishness. Real knowledge comes from the living God. "The fear of the Lord *is* the beginning of knowledge, *but* fools despise wisdom and instruction" (Prov. 1:7).

As Nebuchadnezzar sat on the edge of his glistening throne, Daniel respectfully told him what he dreamed:

> *"You, O king, were watching; and behold, a great image! This great image, whose splendor was excellent, stood before you; and its form was awesome. This image's head was of fine gold, its chest and arms of silver, its belly and thighs of bronze, its legs of iron, its feet partly of iron and partly of clay. You watched while a stone was cut out without hands, which struck the image on its feet of iron and clay, and broke them in pieces. Then the iron, the clay, the bronze, the silver, and the gold were crushed together, and became like chaff from the summer threshing floors; the wind carried them away so that no trace of them was found. And the stone that struck the image became a great mountain and filled the whole earth. **This is the dream...**"* (Daniel 2:31-36).

"That's it!" Nebuchadnezzar probably stammered, almost falling off his throne. "What does it mean?" Daniel's reply concerned the entire human race—including sorcerers. His message reaches down to the end of time:

> *"Now we will tell the interpretation of it before the king. You, O king, are a king of kings. For the God of Heaven has given you a kingdom, power, strength, and glory; and wherever the children of men dwell, or the beasts of the field and the birds of the heaven, He has given them into your hand, and has made you ruler over them all—you are this head of gold"* (Daniel 2:36-38).

Daniel said that the golden head on the metallic image Nebuchadnezzar saw in his foggy dream represented the king and his Babylonian kingdom. In the *Harry Potter* books, Professor Binns looked back and mingled real history with fantasy. It's time to bypass all fantasy and discover a power-packed biblical prophecy that *looked forward* and predicted world history in advance. You can verify its accuracy in any library.

THE BATTLE: **Prophecies in Conflict**

"You are this head of gold." Historically, Babylon was known for its gold. Nicknamed "the golden city," the poet Aeschylus (525-456 B.C.) said it was "teeming with gold." The famous Greek historian Herodotus (484-425 B.C.) visited Babylon around 90 years after Nebuchadnezzar's era and wondered at the amount of gold in the city. Babylon's walls and buildings glistened with gold. Entering the Ishtar Gate and walking down Procession Street would take a visitor to the Temple of Marduk (Babylon's main god) that supported a 40-foot golden statue of Marduk rising near a golden chair, golden table, and golden altar. Thus, Daniel's words to Nebuchadnezzar, "You are this head of gold," fit perfectly.

King Nebuchadnezzar was Babylon's primary builder (see Dan. 4:30). He hoped his golden empire would last forever, but it was not to be. The Jewish prophet continued:

"But after you shall arise another kingdom inferior to yours; then another, a third kingdom of bronze, which shall rule over all the earth" (Daniel 2:39).

Here Daniel revealed "the secret" that Nebuchadnezzar's dream was really a *prophecy* of the rise and fall of nations. "After you shall arise another kingdom inferior to yours." So it was. In 538 B.C., Babylonia fell to Persia—a nation represented by the breast and silver arms of the image in Nebuchadnezzar's dream. Historically, Persia was known for its silver. It used silver coins for commerce. "Then another, a third kingdom of bronze...shall rule over all the earth." In 331 B.C., at the battle of Arbela, Alexander the Great mercilessly crushed Persia's army in the name of Greece, even though his troops were outnumbered 20 to 1. Providence was on his side. Prophecy must be fulfilled. The Greeks were known for their brass, fighting their battles with brass swords and shields.

"And the fourth kingdom shall be as strong as iron, inasmuch as iron breaks in pieces and shatters everything; and like iron

that crushes, that kingdom will break in pieces and crush all the others" (Daniel 2:40).

History confirms perfectly that the fourth kingdom after Babylon, Persia, and Greece, was Rome, the mightiest of them all. The famed historian Edward Gibbon (1737-1794), in his classic, *History of the Decline and Fall of the Roman Empire*, even used the exact language of biblical prophecy when he wrote about "the iron monarchy of Rome":

> The arms of the [Roman] Republic, sometimes vanquished in battle, always victorious in war, advanced with rapid steps to the Euphrates, the Danube, the Rhine, and the ocean; and the images of gold, or silver, or brass, that might serve to represent the nations and their kings, were successively broken by the iron monarchy of Rome.[4]

Roman Caesars ruled the civilized world from 168 B.C. to A.D. 476, until the imperial government finally crumbled under the vicious assaults of barbarian invaders from the wild territories of northern Germany. From A.D. 476 onward—even to this day—Europe has remained divided, exactly as Nebuchadnezzar's dream predicted.

Daniel told the trembling king:

> *"Whereas you saw the feet and toes, partly of potter's clay and partly of iron, the kingdom shall be divided; yet the strength of the iron shall be in it, just as you saw the iron mixed with ceramic clay"* (Daniel 2:41).

True to the prophecy, between A.D. 351 and A.D. 476, Rome's kingdom was divided into ten smaller nations—Alamani, Burgundians, Anglo-Saxons, Suevi, Visagoths, Lombards, Franks, Vandals, Heruli and Ostrogoths[5]—most of which eventually became the nations of Europe we see today. That one prophetic word, "divided," accurately describes the state of Europe from the fifth century until now.

"And as the toes of the feet were partly of iron and partly of clay, so the kingdom shall be partly strong and partly fragile" (Daniel 2:42).

How true this prophecy is! Some European nations are strong, some are weak. Some are like iron, some are like clay. It's been this way for 1,500 years. Sometimes "the toes" get along, sometimes they don't. Daniel revealed more precise details:

"As you saw iron mixed with ceramic clay, they will mingle with the seed of men..." (Daniel 2:43).

"Mingling with the seed of men" is a prediction of intermarriage among the toes, that is, between various royal houses throughout Europe. The purpose of such mingling was to create alliances so that one toe could finally become the big toe—with the goal in mind of a fully reunited Europe under one government. Simply study European history with its royal weddings, incest, in-laws, and out-laws. It's all predicted in God's Word. Yet for 1,500 years, complete unity has eluded the contestants, for it is written:

"...but they will not adhere to one another, just as iron does not mix with clay" (Daniel 2:43).

So it has been; so it is now. Throughout European history various kings, generals, and dictators have tried to unite Europe under their rule, but they all failed. Charlemagne tried it. Charles V tried it. So did Louis XIV, Kaiser Wilhelm, Napoleon Bonaparte, and Adolf Hitler. Yet Europe remains splintered because *God's prophecy* predicts, "they will *not* adhere to one another, just as iron does *not* mix with clay."

Napoleon knew about the prophecy in Daniel 2. When the Little Corporal was finally defeated at the Battle of Waterloo, he purportedly said, "God Almighty is too much for me!" During the rise of the Third Reich, Adolf Hitler became ill. While lying upon his sickbed, his attending nurse showed him Nebuchadnezzar's dream. "It doesn't fit into my plans!" the dictator shouted, throwing the Bible against the wall. But Hitler's cruelty didn't fit into God's plans, and a bullet from his own gun finally ended his miserable life.

King Nebuchadnezzar couldn't possibly have foreseen all this, but the One who revealed His secret to Daniel surely did. In the hearing of the awestruck king, the Jewish prophet swiftly approached his climax:

> *"And in the days of these kings the God of Heaven will set up a kingdom which shall never be destroyed; and the kingdom shall not be left to other people; it shall break in pieces and consume all these kingdoms, and it shall stand forever"* (Daniel 2:44).

After the rise and fall of Babylonia, Persia, Greece, and Rome, after centuries of European intermarriage and division, and after all efforts for complete unity have miserably failed, "the God of heaven will set up a kingdom which shall never be destroyed." This Kingdom won't have a beginning and ending date to be recorded in some history book. Neither will it take its place beside *any human government* in some sort of cooperative, legal relationship. No. "It shall break in pieces and consume all these kingdoms, and it shall stand for ever."

The metal man in Nebuchadnezzar's dream represents the kingdoms of men. At the end of his dream, the golden head, silver arms, bronze belly, iron legs, and divided toes are consumed and obliterated entirely. God's kingdom alone will remain. "It shall stand forever."

Looking the Babylonian monarch squarely in the eyes (which were probably quite wide by now), the Jewish prophet concluded:

> *"Inasmuch as you saw that the stone was cut out of the mountain without hands, and that it broke in pieces the iron, the bronze, the clay, the silver, and the gold—the great God has made known to the king what will come to pass after this. The dream is certain, and its interpretation is sure"* (Daniel 2:45).

The multi-mineral statue is crushed by "the stone" representing God's kingdom. That boulder is quarried from a mountain, "without hands," meaning no human influence is involved. It is wholly divine: A Rock of Ages. The prophecy comes from "the great God who has made known to the king what will come to pass after this." No speculation is involved. This prediction doesn't come from some scary ghost speaking through an unconscious medium in a trance, or from any "harsh voice" hissing from the "other side" (as in Professor Trelawney's message to Albus Dumbledore). No; it comes *from God*, as explained by his true prophet. "The dream is certain, and its interpretation sure." Period.

> *Then King Nebuchadnezzar fell on his face, prostrate before Daniel, and commanded that they should present an offering and incense to him. The king answered Daniel, and said, "Truly your God is the God of gods, the Lord of kings, and a revealer of secrets, since you could reveal this secret." Then the king promoted Daniel and gave him many great gifts; and he made him ruler over the whole province of Babylon, and chief administrator over all the wise men of Babylon* (Daniel 2:46-48).

Nebuchadnezzar recognized truth when he heard it. The Holy Spirit unlocked his heart to acknowledge the Source and Interpreter of his dream: God Almighty, One above all magicians, astrologers, sorcerers, fortune-tellers, or palm readers.

Before concluding this chapter, there's one more section in the Book of Revelation we'll zero in on. It's about Babylon; not the ancient one, but its apocalyptic counterpart. John called it, "MYSTERY, BABYLON THE GREAT, THE MOTHER OF HARLOTS AND OF ABOMINATIONS OF THE EARTH" (Rev. 17:5). Before this seductive mistress is pulverized with the rest of the earth's nations by Heaven's descending Rock, Revelation pinpoints one major element of her wiles—sorcery. Notice carefully:

> *The light of a lamp shall not shine in you anymore, and the voice of the bridegroom and bride shall not be heard in you anymore. For your merchants were the great men of the*

earth, **for by your sorcery all the nations were deceived** (Revelation 18:23).

Revelation 18:23 describes God's last appeal to mixed-up humans before Mystery Babylon goes down. "The light of a lamp" is the illuminating light of the Bible itself, for David said to God, "Your word is a lamp to my feet and a light to my path" (Ps. 119:105). "The voice of the bridegroom" is the tender, pleading voice of Jesus Christ, our heavenly Lover. "The bride" is His Church (see Rev. 19:7-8). Before the end strikes like a whirlwind, God and His Church try to shed the radiant light of Scripture into Mystery Babylon's darkest recesses, but she refuses to listen. Instead, she chooses sorcery, and deceives the world with the same. *"For by your sorcery all the nations were deceived."* At last the heavenly voice fades into eternal night, and is heard no more.

We've seen that magical arts were practiced in ancient Babylon and noted that Nebuchadnezzar's wise men were "magicians...astrologers...[and] sorcerers" (Dan. 2:2). In fact, if you study history's dusty records carefully, you'll discover that much of the world's occultism—both ancient and modern—originated with Babylon. The Bible also confirms that one reason why all that's left of Nebuchadnezzar's empire is sun-dried bricks is "because of the multitude of [her] *sorceries* [and] the great abundance of [her] *enchantments*" (Isa. 47:9). According to the Book of Revelation—which draws most of its imagery from the Old Testament—these same delusions will saturate Planet Earth before the Second Coming of Jesus Christ. *For by your sorcery were all nations deceived.*

Revelation 18:23 is part of God's "sure word of prophecy" (2 Pet. 1:19 KJV). The prediction is non-fiction, earnest, and real. It warns of real sorcery deceiving "the nations"—the same nations filled with kids who love *Harry Potter* (those books are being read in over 200 countries), and who are being desensitized to the occult by J.K. Rowling's subtle witchcraft-made-funny novels. In these end-times, *prophecies are in conflict*. There are true predictions originating from God (such as in Daniel 2), and false prophecies being channeled by misled humans inspired by the devil. *Harry Potter* is mostly fiction, but J.K. Rowling's detailed description of Professor Trelawney's "prophecy" mirrors what's happening right now behind closed doors (or on TV) in real-life occult circles. Don't be fooled. All "channeled" prophecies originate with lucifer and rebel angels. They're part of "Mystery Babylon" and the kingdoms of man.

The prophecy of Nebuchadnezzar's metallic image reveals we're in the toenails of time. Heaven's Rock will soon pulverize all satanic arts.

"The dream is certain, and its interpretation is sure" (Dan. 2:45).

ENDNOTES

1. Rowling, *Order of the Phoenix*, pp. 839-840.

2. Rowling, *Order of the Phoenix*, pp. 841-844.

3. Rowling, *Prisoner of Azkaban*, p. 324.

4. Edward Gibbon, *The History of the Decline and Fall of the Roman Empire*, Vol. III, Chap. 38, p. 634 (1776-1788), found under "General Observations of the Fall of the Roman Empire in the West." See http://www.fordham.edu/halsall/source/gibbon-fall.html.

5. Alonzo Jones, *Ecclesiastical Empire* (Battle Creek, MI: Review and Herald Publishing Association, 1901), chapters 2-7, 12, 13.

CHAPTER 15

THE ALTERNATIVE:

The Man With Scars

*The greatest thing about any civilization is the human person,
and the greatest thing about any person is the possibility
of his encounter with the person of Jesus Christ.*
—Charles Malik

Wicca witchcraft claims to offer kids, teens, and grown-ups magical powers, an ability to cope, and a degree of personal fulfillment inaccessible to the average Joe (uninitiated Muggles). Supposedly, these perks come via occult techniques that enable trained witches to tap into hidden power sources—energies within nature, impulses from spirits, deities, gods, the goddess, or from divinity within. Essentially, that's what Harry Potter's life is all about. He's a young wizard-in-training studying occult technique at Hogwarts who becomes increasingly powerful through learning the complex arts of the Craft.

As a parent, one of my core convictions is that if we take something away from a child because it isn't good for them, we should replace it with something better. We shouldn't just condemn, resist, and avoid the negative, but should embrace, highlight, and promote the positive. In this light we inquire: Is there a wholesome and uplifting alternative to both *Harry Potter* and real witchcraft that can capture the attention of young people, provide dynamic power to cope with life's stresses, and above all, satisfy the human heart's deepest longings for love and affection? Yes, there is, and it's been around for centuries. Correction: Eternity. It's not a thing, a book, or a fairy tale—although the most fantastic stories have been written—but a Person. His name is Jesus Christ.

Immediately after commanding Israel not to "learn" abominable occult practices (see Deut. 18:9-14), Moses predicted:

> *The Lord your God will raise up for you a Prophet like me*
> *from your midst, from your brethren. Him you shall hear*
> (Deuteronomy 18:15).

In Acts 3:19-26 Peter specifically applied the above prediction to Jesus Christ, through whom "all the families of the earth shall be blessed" (Acts 3:25). Therefore, when we compare Deuteronomy 18:9-15 with Acts 3:19-26, we discover that *Jesus Christ* is Heaven's alternative to witchcraft, sorcery, spells, and potions.

Scott Cunningham, author of *The Truth About Witchcraft*, contends:

> Perhaps it's not too strong to say that the highest form of
> human vanity is the assumption that your religion is the only
> way to the Deity, that everyone will find it as fulfilling as you
> do, and that those with different beliefs are deluded, misled,
> or ignorant.[1]

Mr. Cunningham's statement is true when applied to man-made religions—but *not* to real Christianity. The true religion of Jesus Christ doesn't spring from man, and it certainly doesn't cater to human vanity (for it sinks man's pride in the dust). Instead, it comes from God Himself. The Bible says:

> *For God so loved the world that He gave His only begotten*
> *Son, that whoever believes in Him should not perish but have*
> *eternal life* (John 3:16).

THE ALTERNATIVE: The Man With Scars

Notice: *God* so loved the world, *God* gave His Son, and *God* now promises everlasting life to believers in Jesus. Is this really true? That's the question.

Biblical Christianity has something no other religion can offer—proof of its claims through credible, historical, prophetic fulfillment. Wicca witchcraft can't touch this. Neither can Islam, Hinduism, or Buddhism. There simply aren't any prophecies in the Koran, Vedas, Buddhist writings, or New Age works predicting definite events that have literally been fulfilled in real history. But Christianity has them. Here's some evidence:

- **1451 B.C.**—Moses predicted the arrival of a "Prophet" (Deut. 18:15). *Fulfilled in Acts 3:19-26.*

- **771 B.C.**—Isaiah predicted this Promised One would live in the vicinity of "Galilee of the Gentiles" and would bring "great light" to those who "dwell in the land of the shadow of death" (Isa. 9:1-2). *Fulfilled in Matthew 4:12-17.*

- **710 B.C.**—Micah predicted this Coming One would be born in "Bethlehem," a tiny town "among the thousands [of cities] of Judah" (Mic. 5:2). *Fulfilled in Matthew 2:1.*

- **538 B.C.**—Daniel predicted this long-awaited "Messiah the Prince" would appear publicly near the close of a 490-year prophecy (Dan. 9:24-27). *Fulfilled in Mark 1:14-15.*

- **487 B.C.**—Zechariah predicted this future "King" would humbly ride into Jerusalem on a donkey (see Zech. 9:9). *Fulfilled in Matthew 21:1-11.*

- **487 B.C.**—Zechariah also predicted He would be betrayed for "thirty pieces of silver" (Zech. 11:12-13). *Fulfilled in Matthew 27:3-10.*

- **1020 B.C.**—David predicted this Divine Sufferer would be rejected, would have His hands and feet pierced (which is what happens when a man is executed by crucifixion), and that wicked men would cast lots for His clothes (see Ps. 22:16-18). *Fulfilled in Matthew 27:35.*

• **712 B.C.**—Isaiah predicted this Suffering Servant would be despised, rejected, would become a prisoner, would bear the world's sin, suffer, die, be buried in the tomb of a rich man, and then rise again from the dead (see Isa. 53:3,6,8-11). *Fulfilled in Matthew 16:23; 27:57; 28:1-8.*

Hundreds of years after these prophecies were originally given they were perfectly fulfilled by Jesus Christ—in His birth, sinless life, intense sufferings, prophesied death, and glorious resurrection. The risen One declared to eyewitnesses of these events:

"O foolish ones, and slow of heart to believe in all that the prophets have spoken! Ought not the Christ to have suffered these things and to enter into His glory?" And beginning at Moses and all the Prophets, He expounded to them in all the Scriptures the things concerning Himself. "Thus it is written, and thus it was necessary for the Christ to suffer and to rise from the dead the third day, and that repentance and forgiveness of sins should be preached in His name to all nations, beginning at Jerusalem. And you are witnesses of these things. Behold, I send the Promise of My Father upon you; but tarry in the city of Jerusalem until you are endued with power from on high" (Luke 24:25-26; 46-49).

The Good News of Jesus Christ's suffering, death, and resurrection (in perfect fulfillment of biblical prophecies) is to be preached to all nations by His followers. *This is Operation Rescue Sinners.* When we respond to God's love and forsake our sins, Jesus Christ freely forgives us by His grace. Then comes the power—not the power of nature, self, gods, the goddess, or spirits—but *"the power* of the Holy Spirit" (Acts 1:8; 2:1-14; Rom. 15:13) to counteract error and advance God's cause.

Jesus Christ tenderly speaks to each of us, pleading:

*Come to Me, all you who labor and are heavy laden, and I will give you rest. Take My yoke upon you, and **learn from Me**, for I am gentle and lowly in heart, and you will find rest for your souls"* (Matthew 11:28-29).

Jesus invites us to "learn" *from Him*, which also means learning *about Him* in order to become *like Him* in character—pure, meek and lowly in heart. When children read *Harry Potter* and watch those movies, what are they learning? Perhaps a few good things about cooperation, stamina, fair play, and unity, but they're also learning about witches, wizards, sorcery, wands, spells, cauldrons, potions, divination, fortune-telling, amulets, talismans, astrology, moral relativism, rule breaking, fits of rage, talking back to parents, temper tantrums, lying, drinking alchohol, smoking pipes, gambling, swearing, cursing, and about a "cool" wizard-boy wearing a fang earring dressed like a rock star—*none of which are presented as wrong or sinful.*

When Jesus said, "Learn from Me, for I am meek and lowly in heart," He wasn't only encouraging focused attention on His perfect life, but He was also teaching this basic lesson: What we learn about molds our character into the image of what we contemplate. Paul taught this truth when he wrote that by "beholding" we are "transformed into the same image" (2 Cor. 3:18) of what we see.

Should the life of Jesus be interesting to youth? *Most definitely.* In fact, there's no life more intriguing, captivating, inspiring, and worth contemplating than that of Him who was born of a virgin, who had no human father, who was born to die in fulfillment of ancient prophecies, who walked lonely paths, was misunderstood by most, who loved His enemies, was betrayed by a friend, became hell's target, cast out devils, told parables, healed the sick, stilled storms, walked on water, met with angels, sweat blood, stood silent before His accusers, endured being spiked to a tree, was enveloped in darkness, forgave a dying thief, whose death was marked by an earthquake, who lay dead for three days, and who burst forth from a cold and clammy grave—alive! Uninteresting?

189

Boring? Come on! If kids think His story is dry, they've been watching too much TV.

"Learn of Me," says the Humble and Unselfish One to self-centered children, cocky youth, searching young adults, mixed-up grown-ups, and hard-hearted elderly persons at death's door. "Learn of Me," He says to witches, sorcerers, palm readers, mediums, astrologers, and fortune-tellers. "Learn of Me," He pleads to those pursuing magical power apart from their Creator and who are foolishly warring against His legitimate sovereignty. "Learn of Me," says the Truth to those duped by satan's lies, "and you shall find rest for your souls." Peace, happiness, fulfillment, and yes—even unspeakable excitement come from the Risen Lover, not from lucifer, spirits, self, sin, or the Craft.

One of the appeals of *Harry Potter* is that Harry's an orphan, an underdog, who battles overwhelming odds. Kids are drawn to this, especially if they're among those unfortunate enough to grow up without the guidance of a loving earthly father or mother. To all bruised young people who need a true friend to lean on, Jesus promises, "*I will not leave you orphans; I will come to you*" (John 14:18). He's the Friend of the friendless.

God commands parents to instill His words deep into their kid's hearts. "You shall teach them diligently to your children," says the Lord (Deut. 6:6-7). Therefore, I recommend the Bible. It speaks of fantastic things—like Heaven, a Celestial City, and a New Earth where lions are as tame as kittens (see Isa. 65:17,25). It's not fiction, and it doesn't give kids nightmares like *Harry Potter and the Goblet of Fire* (believe me, that book has many scary scenes). True, its pages may not be as mesmerizing as *The Prisoner of Azkaban*, yet it describes a wonderful future that will be a lot more fun than the most thrilling Warner Brothers flick about Harry and Hogwarts.

If you want to read good fiction, I also recommend the immortal classic, *The Pilgrim's Progress*, by John Bunyan (written in 1684, but still available at most bookstores). Modern youth need the character lessons in that book more than imaginary portrayals of broomstick wizard sports. *The Pilgrim's Progress* is an allegory about a young man named Christian who, after leaving the City of Destruction, embarks on a dangerous trek toward the Celestial City (representing Heaven). En route, he encounters dangers on every hand (like kids do today) and learns patience, humility, purity, honesty, and faith in God—virtues entirely absent in *Harry Potter*. He meets friends (like Prudence, Piety, Hopeful, and Faithful), and foes (such as Worldly Wise Man, Ignorance, Flatterer, Vain Confidence, and Giant Despair of Doubting Castle). Christian also discovers how to get rid of a terrible burden on his back. After climbing a steep and rugged hill, he sees an uplifted cross with God's Son hanging there. Gazing in faith, his heavy burden falls off his back and rolls down the hill. He's free through the grace of Jesus Christ!

As Christian meanders along the Narrow Way, he meets a hideous, scaly fiend named Apollyon (representing satan), and after a fierce battle, finally pierces its devilish heart with his sword (representing the Bible), delivering the death blow. Of course, *The Pilgrim's Progress* is also fiction, yet for over 300 years it has inspired youth to forsake sin and live upright, righteous lives by God's grace.

In the very first *Harry Potter* book, when Lord Voldemort propelled his death-curse against baby Harry, it bounced back, searing a lightning-shaped scar into the child's face. Albus Dumbledore remarked to a fellow wizard:

"He'll have that scar forever."[2]

Of course, this is total fantasy. Almost 2,000 ago, just outside of Jerusalem, Jesus Christ was brutally assaulted by the real Dark One and beaten by the very human beings He came to save. His hands and feet were spiked to a tree. Before His dying breath, His tender heart experienced the full curse of this world's sin—the sin of pride, "the sin of witchcraft" (1 Sam. 15:23), the sin of pursuing magical power apart from the Creator, and the horrible guilt of every other perverse thought and action.

There's only one kind of power God wants flowing through us. It's safe, friendly, and grounded in truth. It's the same power that compelled

Jesus to come down from Heaven and to humble Himself "to the point of death, even the death of the cross" (Phil. 2:8). It's the power of love—of God's infinite love for us—now revealed through "the power of the Holy Spirit" (Rom. 15:13) and the tears of the Crucified One.

Jesus is the Man With Scars. As far as we know, He'll forever bear the marks of Roman nails on His hands and feet.

He thinks we were worth the price.

ENDNOTES

1. Cunningham, *The Truth About Witchcraft*, p. 48.
2. Rowling, *Sorcerer's Stone*, p. 32.

CHAPTER 16

THE MOTIVATION:
Love's Chamber of Secrets

Love is a force more formidable than any other.
It is invisible — it cannot be seen or measured, yet
it is powerful enough to transform you in a moment, and
offer you more joy than any material possession could.
—Barbara De Angelis, American Author
Expert on Relationships

Our first son, Seth Michael Wohlberg, was scheduled to arrive on August 15, 2004. Because complications developed in my wife Kristin's pregnancy, Seth came three weeks early. This is our story.

During the week of July 19-23, I was conducting a prophecy seminar before an eager crowd about two hours north of our home in Paso Robles, California. The town where the meetings were held was coastal Soquel, near Monterey. Wednesday afternoon, July 21, at about 4:20 P.M., a woman from the audio-video booth walked onto the platform and handed me a note, unexpectedly interrupting my talk.

"Your wife's in the hospital, call immediately!" it said. Jolted, I switched off my wireless microphone and stuttered, "Err...ah... Doesn't she know I'm teaching right now? Please call the hospital for me. If it's an emergency, I'll come right away." With that, I tried to regain my composure and continue my talk entitled, *"Seven Years of Tribulation?"* My tribulation had begun! The audience waited anxiously to see what might unfold.

I knew Kristin had seen her OB-GYN for her regular pre-natal exam that morning. I also knew the nurse had detected a slight irregularity in Seth's heart rate and had scheduled Kristin for two hours of fetal monitoring that afternoon at Twin Cities Community Hospital in Templeton. I knew all that, which made us both nervous. What I didn't know was that once at the hospital, soon after being connected to the monitor, Kristin began having major contractions up to four minutes in length. Seth's heart rate ominously dropped from the normal range of about 150 beats per minute to 90. Nurses rushed in and quickly slapped an oxygen mask over Kristin's mouth, which terrified her, for she hadn't felt any contractions at all! Seth's heart rate stabilized. Someone called the Soquel auditorium to notify me. That's when the lady handed me the note.

About 15 minutes after the woman went back to the audio-video booth to phone the hospital, one of the TV screens in front of me began flashing furiously, *Labor Now! Labor Now!* "Oh my!" I blurted out in shock. "I...I've gotta go! My wife's in labor!" Sweating, anxious, happy, and confused, this dad-to-be dashed out of the auditorium as fast as possible. Two and a half hours later I was at Kristin's side. It was now Wednesday evening. We stayed at the hospital all night while nurses monitored Seth's heart rate continually. Now we were both extremely nervous, for we had no idea how long Kristin had been having unfelt contractions, how many times our baby's heart rate had dropped during the past week, and whether there had been any oxygen deprivation to his tiny brain.

Thursday morning the doctors gave Kristin a drug to induce labor while watching Seth's heart rate constantly. Her contractions continued, with some still as long as four minutes (normal contractions last less than a minute). Seth's heart rate weathered the long contractions pretty well, yet sometimes dropped down again below the safety zone. Seeing this, our primary doctor (Dr. Thomas, a wonderful man) decided to re-move Seth as soon as possible. A C-section was scheduled for that very night at 5:30 P.M. Wow! Our heads were spinning. Was Seth okay? Kristin's pregnancy was just shy of 37 weeks, so technically, Seth wasn't quite full term. No matter, he was slated for birth within hours.

Running a bit late, nurses took Kristin at 6:30 P.M. for anesthesia. I was brought into the operating room at about 7:00. In the room was Dr. Thomas, nine nurses, plus the two of us. The mood was positive and upbeat. What happened next seemed unbelievable. A sheet blocked Kristin's view so she couldn't see the full procedure. After comforting her, I went to the other side of the sheet and saw the incision. Soon a tiny head popped out of my wife's abdomen. Seth was facing away from me. "I'm turning his head around," Dr. Thomas said cheerfully. I watched in awe, trying to look and focus my camera at the same time (four nurses stood behind me in case I fainted). As soon as Dr. Thomas turned Seth's face toward me, he shouted, "Push!" Then one nurse pushed hard on Kristin's stomach.

Within seconds Seth flew out like a missile, arms waving wildly! He took one breath and screamed with full vigor! I have never seen anything like it. Quickly they cut his umbilical cord and placed him on a table next to me. There he lay, squirming frantically, our son, fully formed, with all ten toes and fingers, looking like the most beautiful baby in the world. "Seth, it's me, your daddy, everything's okay!" Im-mediately Seth stopped crying, put his little hands on his mouth, and listened hard to a voice he'd heard many times (we had read Bible sto-ries and talked to him a lot). I ran back around the sheet to Kristin and said, "Honey, he looks great! I'll be right back!" Rushing over to Seth, the doctor let me cut a smaller portion of umbilical cord. The nurses cleaned Seth up a bit and I carried him around the sheet to show Kristin as our tears flowed.

It was then my privilege to carry Seth down the hallway to the nursery where some of our friends waited anxiously. A friendly pedia-trician examined our little boy, and said with a smile, "Congratulations.

You have a very healthy baby!" He was 6 pounds, 15 ounces; and 20 inches long. Alive and kicking!

For many years the thought of having a child was scary to me. Too much responsibility. Some friends said things like, "Better enjoy your freedom now," "A baby's a new boss," or, "Your life will change forever!" When they said, "change forever," this didn't sound so good. But when Seth popped out, everything did change, and the change was fantastic. Others said, "You won't believe the depth of love you'll feel for your child—nothing compares to it." They were right.

I've always dreaded the idea of changing smelly diapers, but believe it or not, I love changing Seth's. What a shock. I actually enjoy laying him on the changing table, slipping off his little "onesie" (a one-piece garment), removing his diaper, and cleaning him up. Tiny hands, small feet, wondering eyes, puckered lips—what a treasure. His first smile pierced our hearts.

Why am I telling you all this? Why include this Seth section in a book about *Harry Potter*, spells, and witchcraft? I include it because of the deep spiritual lessons I've learned through Seth's birth—about God's love, His personal nature, and the depth of His sacrifice in giving His Son to die on a cross for our sins.

First lesson: God's personal nature. Witchcraft teaches, "There is a power in the universe. It is the power of life. This is the inexplicable force behind the wonders that the early humans encountered. The Earth, the solar system, the stars—all that's manifest—is a product of this power."[1] As we've already seen, Wicca says this power is "neither positive nor negative, neither good nor evil."[2] Hogwarts! (I mean, *Hogwash*.) *Nothing* could be further from the truth.

Seth's little body wasn't meticulously formed inside Kristin by a non-personal flow of mindless, cosmic energy. It wasn't some "inexplicable force" that fashioned his complex brain, functioning liver, lungs, kidneys, eyes, nose, ears—or those heart-melting smiles. Impossible! Pondering the miracle of conception, pregnancy, birth, and life, David said to God:

THE MOTIVATION: **Love's Chamber of Secrets**

*For You formed my inward parts; You wove me in my mother's womb. I will praise You, for I am fearfully and wonderfully made; marvelous are Your works, and that **my soul knows very well**"* (Psalm 139:13-14).

So does mine. God is a highly personal Creator who "formed" our "inward parts" in our "mother's womb." When Seth was born, this truth penetrated my heart powerfully.

Second Lesson: God's Love, as Kristin and I watch our baby boy grow (he's now three months old), our love for him grows, too. "He's so cute. I can hardly stand it!" my wife often says. As we ponder the depth of our love for Seth, we're led to think more seriously about where such love comes from. We know the answer. "He who does not love does not know God, for *God is love*" (1 John 4:8). God is Creator and Lover—the Source of love.

Third Lesson: Gazing at little Seth, as any parent would, I long to protect him from the big bad world around us. For nearly nine months he was safe inside Kristin; now he's out, exposed to potential pain, cruelty, temptation, and sin. There's nothing I wouldn't do to preserve him from harm. After Seth's birth, I thought: *Would I be willing to sacrifice my child to save a lost world, most of which could not care less?* Suddenly, the Bible's most famous verse throbbed with new meaning:

*For God so loved the world that **He gave His only begotten Son**, that whoever believes in Him should not perish, but have everlasting life* (John 3:16).

God gave His Son—He sacrificed Him. He not only allowed Jesus to leave Heaven's safety zone to be born into our dark world of sin, but He permitted Him to be despised and rejected by men, attacked by satan, crushed in Gethsemane under the weight of this world's wickedness, forsaken by friends, tried by some Jews and Romans, stripped, whipped, crucified, mocked, and finally to be left trembling in darkness under the full curse of His broken Law's irrevocable penalty—death.

197

Our Heavenly Father permitted all this to happen to His Son. Why? Because hidden deep within His Being is a "chamber of secrets"—a heart filled with more love than we can possibly imagine. Contrary to witchcraft's philosophy (and the teaching of many religions), God isn't an impersonal force that's neither positive nor negative, neither good nor evil. For proof, *just look at the cross!* Now that Seth's here, I can hardly fathom what the Father must have felt when, looking sorrowfully from Heaven, He beheld this horrible scene and heard His Son's scream.

> *Now from the sixth hour to the ninth hour there was darkness over all the land. And about the ninth hour Jesus cried out with a loud voice, saying, "Eli, Eli, lama sabachthani?" that is, "My God, My God, why have You forsaken Me?"* (Matthew 27:45-46)

Operation Rescue Sinners was painful—more painful than we can possibly imagine. The Father and His Son endured a searing separation because of our sins. They did it because they love each of us—because they love *you.* Love's "Chamber of Secrets"—their hearts—has been opened. They hope this revelation of their love will penetrate other chambers—our hearts—compelling us to surrender our lives to Jesus Christ without reservation.

What holds people back? Just one primary word: Self. Although we may not practice *witchcraft,* we all have the same root problem: *Selfcraft.* Whenever we say "no," "not now," or "maybe later" to God, we put ourselves in lucifer's camp.

" 'The truth,' Albus Dumbledore sighed, 'It is a very beautiful and terrible thing.'"[3] Yes, it is. But the greatest truth is not in *Harry Potter,* Wicca witchcraft, or any other man-made religion. It's in what the Heavenly Father and His Son willingly suffered to save us from sin.

Have *you* responded to their love?

Why not yield *your heart* today?

ENDNOTES

1. Cunningham, *The Truth About Witchcraft Today*, pp. 19-20.
2. Cunningham, *The Truth About Witchcraft Today*, p. 39.
3. Rowling, *Sorcerer's Stone*, p. 298.

CHAPTER 17

THE PROTECTION:

Defense Against the Dark Arts

Put on the whole armor of God, that you may
be able to stand against the wiles of the devil.

(Ephesians 6:11)

"**W**hat is your name?" (Mark 5:9) Jesus Christ fearlessly asked the naked, wild-eyed, demon-possessed lunatic who inhabited cemeteries. "My name is Legion; for we are many," snarled back a host of devils through their captured victim's contorted lips. What a sight for Christ's disciples to behold! The superior power of God's Son was restraining a murderous, crazy man whose body was indwelt by demons.

> *A large herd of swine was feeding there near the mountains.*
> *So all the demons begged Him, saying, "Send us to the swine,*
> *that we may enter them." And at once Jesus gave them per-*
> *mission. Then the unclean spirits went out and entered the*
> *swine (there were about two thousand); and the herd ran vi-*
> *olently down the steep place into the sea, and drowned in the*
> *sea. So those who fed the swine fled, and they told it in the*
> *city and in the country. And they went out to see what it was*
> *that had happened. Then they came to Jesus, and saw the one*

201

who had been demon-possessed and had the legion, sitting and clothed and in his right mind (Mark 5:11-15).

This is only one of many accounts recorded in the New Testament of evil spirits taking possession of human beings—and then being driven out by Jesus Christ. In each situation, demonic spirits are presented as real, intelligent, strong, and destructive. Many people rationalize away this ominous reality, but how can one explain 2,000 pigs being forced into the sea?

Here are two more examples:

Then they went into Capernaum, and immediately on the Sabbath He entered the synagogue and taught...Now there was a man in their synagogue with an unclean spirit. And he cried out, saying, "Let us alone! What have we to do with You, Jesus of Nazareth? Did You come to destroy us? I know who You are—the Holy One of God!" But Jesus rebuked him, saying, "Be quiet, and come out of him!" And when the unclean spirit had convulsed him and cried out with a loud voice, he came out of him (Mark 1:21-26).

Then one of the crowd answered and said, "Teacher, I brought You my son, who has a mute spirit. And whenever it seizes him, it throws him down; he foams at the mouth, gnashes his teeth, and becomes rigid. So I spoke to Your disciples, that they should cast it out, but they could not." He answered him and said, "O faithless generation, how long shall I be with you? How long shall I bear with you? Bring him to Me." Then they brought him to Him. And when he saw Him, immediately the spirit convulsed him, and he fell on the ground and wallowed, foaming at the mouth. So He asked his father, "How long has this been happening to him?" And he said, "From childhood. And often he has thrown him both into the fire and into the water to destroy him. But if You can do anything, have compassion on us and help us."...When Jesus saw that the people came running together, He rebuked the unclean spirit, saying to it: "Deaf and dumb spirit, I command you, come out of him and enter him no more!" Then the spirit cried out, convulsed him greatly, and came out of him (Mark 9:17-22, 25-26).

As we've already seen, Wicca witches don't believe satan exists; neither do they believe in demonic spirits. Thus they reject the Scripture's testimony as to the reality, organization, and malicious power of fallen angels—which makes them highly vulnerable to being silently invaded and possessed by these very forces. The Bible says we're contending against a vast array of "principalities [and] powers, against the rulers of the darkness of this age, against spiritual *hosts* of wickedness in the heavenly *places*" (Eph. 6:12). Lucifer's legions aren't imaginary, or harmless.

To be fair, those who consider themselves "white" witches *do* believe there are evil witches, unfriendly deities, haunting spirits of the dead, and other less-than-desirable entities floating around Earth's atmosphere from which they need protection. In the *Potter* series, a course is even offered at Hogwarts that teaches young wizards about such protection. It's called: *Defense Against the Dark Arts.*

The class everyone was looking forward to was Defense Against the Dark Arts...There was so much to learn...[1]

In Defense classes, Harry, Ron, Fred, George, Hermione, and other Hogwarts students learn about protective spells designed to ward off evil. When it became known that Voldemort was regaining his powers, Hermione nervously wanted more than preliminary knowledge:

[Hermione] paused, looked sideways at Harry, and went on. "And by that I mean learning how to defend ourselves properly, not just theory, but the real spells...I want to be properly trained in defense because...because..." She took a great breath and finished. "Because Lord Voldemort's back."[2]

Again fantasy is mixed with reality. The idea of using good spells to fight bad spells is real witchcraft philosophy. The same teaching is in *Teen Witch: Wicca for a New Generation*. Chapter 5 of *Teen Witch* is entitled, "Spells Just for You." Silver Ravenwolf naively reports:

> Spells fall into five basic categories: Love, Health, Money, Protection, and Other (a catchall for spells that don't seem to fit anywhere else). Each category has its own set of rules. As I write this, I think lovingly of my own children and how, over the years, I've taught them spellcasting techniques. A little here, a bit there, until they have gained quite a repertoire of their own spellcasting techniques. I can tell you that when my own children put their minds to the task, they can out-spell any adept Witch on the face of the planet.[3]

For protective magick, Silver recommends various techniques utilizing the supposed powers of "the moon (protection for women and children); Mars (when we have to turn negativity back quickly)... Venus (when we wish to flood a situation with love rather than negative energies); and Saturn (when we banish a difficulty or wish to push something negative away from us)." Other spells seek protection through colors, "white (purity of Spirit); black (to banish); blue-black (for healing and protection); dark purple (for calling our ancestors to help); indigo blue (astral projection, truth, and defense)..." et cetera. Then there's the supposedly supportive influence of fruits, vegetables, herbs, and plants. At last, help comes from "the four elements":

> Earth to stabilize our foundations and hide our treasures; Air to push negative people or situations away from us, and to bring protective energy toward us; Fire to blind our enemies with brilliance and heat (too hot to touch) or burn away negative energies that seek to overcome us; Water to transform a bad situation into a good one....[4]

All of this is expected to protect teenage witches and Craft members from any "negative energies" floating around the universe seeking to harm them as they practice "positive" spell casting, cooperate with "good spirits," connect with the "goddess," get help from "ancestors" and "guardian angels," channel Nature's power to accomplish "good" goals, and tap into the divinity they imagine resides within their aging, far-from-perfect bodies. While there is variety, essentially this is Wicca witchcraft, the *Charmed* TV series, the *W.I.T.C.H.* books, the *Daughters of the Moon* novels, *Sweep*, and of course, *Harry Potter*. But, based on what the Scriptures plainly teach, the supernatural power associated with real witchcraft stems from another source entirely. That hidden source is:

> *...according to the working of satan, with all power, signs, and lying wonders, and with all unrighteous deception among those who perish, because they did not receive the love of the truth, that they might be saved. And for this reason God will send them a strong delusion, that they should believe the lie, that they all may be condemned who did not believe the truth, but had pleasure in unrighteousness* (2 Thessalonians 2:9-12).

According to the Bible, Wicca's protection is an illusion, just like the emperor's new clothes, described in the classic children's tale. Tricked by a crafty merchant into paying an exorbitant price for invisible garments that didn't exist, the gullible emperor finally discovered he was naked. It's the same with "white" witchcraft. It offers *no* real protection from "negative energies"—only false security. In fact, because witchcraft rejects God's Word, all of its supposedly enlightened techniques actually invite the presence of satan and his legions, leading to demon possession. The Craft, *Teen Witch*, and even *Harry Potter* may look friendly, but behind the scenes dark realities often intrude.

It happened to Vincent McCann while still a teenager. His testimony, *Set Free From Witchcraft and the Occult: My Story*, is both inspiring and frightening.[5] "I began to practice 'white' witchcraft," Vincent reflects, "and set up an altar in my bedroom." To this curious, searching teen, it "seemed harmless enough," and he was excited about the possibility of "changing things for the better." Vincent soon acquired "quite an interesting array of occult literature" (including Tarot cards), yet he kept much of this hidden because, as he tells us, "I knew that my parents would become offended." He longed to gain "more knowledge about the occult and to obtain power," but he had no clue what kind of power he was toying with.

Vincent become involved with a mysterious young lady named Jane. "She also encouraged my interest in the occult and we performed spells together." Yet as time went on, what started out pleasant turned horrifying:

> Nothing could have prepared me for what happened next. All of a sudden she [Jane] stood up and began pacing up and down the kitchen doing what first appeared to be impersonations. Thinking it was just her way of having a joke I simply laughed it off. But she continued this behavior to the point were it was beyond a joke and I had stopped laughing. There was a point when she looked at me and I could clearly see that I was no longer talking to the same person. She spoke in a male voice and her whole personality had radically changed. The voice professed to be that of a spirit who had indwelt her since early childhood. It threatened me not to tell anyone about its existence and said that if I did so it would kill me, my mother, my father, and my brother.[6]

This young dabbler "watched in sheer terror as a new personality emerged through Jane in such a way that it seemingly rose up from deep within her." Soon "various spirits" spoke through Jane. Once, "She jumped up screaming at the top of her voice and white foam gushed out of her mouth. I had never known such a feeling of absolute terror in all my life."… "I was at the point of feeling as though I was going to have a complete nervous breakdown. I could hardly believe that such things were happening to me." For the first time in Vincent's young life, he realized he was dealing with "dark spiritual forces of evil."[7]

If you want to know all the details, you can read his full testimony. After many more frightening experiences, Vincent decided to visit a Christian church with his brother Kevin. "I couldn't get to the church quick enough!" he confessed. There he heard about "the victory of Jesus Christ over Satan and all the powers of darkness." A song was sung. The words were just for him:

> There's not a fetter that You cannot break Lord, there's not a demon that can stand in Your way Lord, there's not a principality, power nor authority that is not under the feet of our God.

This was exactly what Vincent needed to hear. The climax came when he invited Jesus Christ into his heart and was delivered from inner torment, fear, guilt, and satanic power. Vincent remembers:

> Even though I had been involved in the occult I always felt, like many people today, that I was generally a "good person." I had never murdered anyone, or beaten up old women, or committed armed robbery. I therefore felt I had a good chance with God. Whenever I did something which was "good" I felt as though God must have been looking down on me and awarding me points which would somehow outweigh the bad things that I did, and that I would eventually get to Heaven when I died. However, after the service finished one of the leaders in the church at the time took me aside and explained how each one of us were sinners by nature and that our sin separated us from God. Jesus Christ came as the only perfect man to reconcile fallen humanity back to their relationship with God through His sacrifice on the cross so that when people turn from their sin and put their faith in Him they begin a new life and can have a certainty of eternal life (see 1 John 5:13). As I spoke with this dear friend the realization dawned upon me that I was indeed a sinner. I knew that I had done terrible things in the past and that my mind was full of sinful thoughts. I repeated a simple prayer of faith and repentance to the Lord Jesus Christ repenting of my sin and asking Him to be the Lord of my life. I was urged to pray this prayer with all my heart and I did so with every fiber of my being. Nobody told me to expect anything through such a

prayer and I was not at all prepared for what happened next. I opened my eyes and said, "I feel as though I have found what I have been looking for all my life!" I realized that all of the things that I had been involved in such as the occult, the music I listened to, etc., had been a search in all the wrong places that nearly led me to utter ruin. I experienced such a sensation of love and peace that I could never adequately put it into words. All I can say is that I felt love. There was no doubt about it. It was love in its most pure form. I knew I was saved.[8]

Praise God—what a testimony! Vincent is not the only one to learn firsthand the cruelty of demonic hatred and the superior power of God's Son. I have a friend named Pam who recently escaped from Wicca. A few days before *Hour of the Witch* was finalized, she emailed to me some details of her story. I told her I sensed this was providential and asked if I might include her testimony in this book. Because her experience was so painful, Pam was reluctant to go public with it, but after realizing it might help others struggling with the same things, she wanted to do it.

As we discussed Wicca's growth among teenagers, Pam's response was, "All those kids being sucked into the devil's hands—he must be delighted. They are like lambs to the slaughter." She herself had "books, the wand, the cauldron, the candles, the altar, the jewelry, the runes, everything (thousands of dollars worth)." After embracing Wiccan magic, at age 24, she was "diagnosed with suicidal depression" and was placed in the Mental Health Unit of a nearby hospital. "I tried to kill myself three times, always without telling anyone." After examining her carefully, a noted psychologist said she had a "multiple personality disorder." "It's true," she said, "I did have multiple personalities, but what was their source?" Opening her heart, Pam confessed:

> I think most people are attracted to Wicca for the same reasons I was: the need for power to protect oneself, the need to worship, and especially the need to belong. The insidious part

is that power is actually taken away and the protection you think you're getting is all a facade. Wicca isn't a game to play at. It is pure witchcraft and entirely of the Devil. And this includes astrology, numerology, gods, and goddesses. Even horoscopes are ultimately based in gods and goddesses. There are some who argue that there is white (good) magic and black (evil) magic. That is not true. All witchcraft, all sorcery, all incantations, all rites and ceremonies that invoke gods and goddesses are evil. Very evil. I could always tell when an evil presence was coming over me. It's like all of a sudden your thoughts are dark, your emotions are muted, and you feel like you're all powerful. Pure Wicca holds that there is no evil force, no devil in the world. Clever ploy of the devil...if he doesn't exist, we don't need to worry about him...I know there is real evil out there. The devil grabs on to someone and holds tight. And you know, sometimes that person can't fight for himself or herself. I couldn't... You are right. The internet, the movies, the ominous exponential rise of interest in the occult and witchcraft, and the levels of socially accepted immorality in some of the most "civilized" nations of the world make for an unparalleled opportunity for deceit the devil will not let slip away.... There is a lot more I could tell you about my experience with witchcraft, and some/most is pretty disgusting and abhorrent to Christianity. But there's also a pretty amazing chain of events that took me right from the midst of Wicca to facing Jesus head-on. God's hand has been in my life for a lot of years, but I had no clue.... It hasn't been more than a few weeks since I absolutely turned myself over to Christ.... You know what? It just about overwhelms me when I think about where I've been, and where I am now.... I don't know what else He has planned for me, but whatever it is, I'll do it! Please keep praying for me. Steve, if you want to use any of what I've written, feel free.

Thank you, Pam, for sharing some of your story. "Lord, use Pam's testimony to help others. Give her strength, keep the devil away from her, and bless her richly is my prayer! In Jesus' name, Amen."

To all readers of this book I say, such accounts can be multiplied; you can read some of them yourself on select Christian web sites, such as those of *Ex Witch Ministries, Fill the Void Ministries, SpotLight Ministries*, and others.[9] From these testimonies, we see how evil angels work. "Hello, I'm your pal," demons often say. They can be quite cordial at times, professing deep interest in our enlightenment, just like the snake offered godhood to Eve.

"And no wonder! For satan himself transforms himself into an angel of light" (2 Cor. 11:14). When it suits their infernal purposes, lucifer's fallen comrades speak in soft, friendly tones. But once they gain a foothold, the mask drops, and they show their true colors. They're killers. They want to destroy us, just like they tried to kill Vincent and Pam, and would like to kill everyone else who naively wanders into their alluring webs of deceit.

It should be quite obvious by now that anything even remotely similar to what Harry Potter learned at Hogwarts, such as "Defense Against the Dark Arts," won't work. Neither will Silver Ravenwolf's naïve suggestions about tapping into the protective power of colors, fruits, vegetables, herbs, air, water, fire, and earth. Not a chance. This would be like trying to defend oneself against a militant band of Islamic terrorists with a toothpick. Again, there's absolutely no *real* protection from *real* evil through witchcraft, the occult, or protective spells. This is all satan's science anyway.

So what can we do? How can we protect our families, homes, and hearts from deadly satanic forces? Until Jesus Christ comes, there's no guarantee that even Christians won't get hurt, suffer, or be killed while living on this sin-infected globe. But there's Good News. God is infinitely stronger than satan, and there are practical things we can do to keep evil angels at bay.

Defensive Solution #1: Confess Every Known Sin

The Bible says, "If we confess our sins, He is faithful and just to forgive us our sins, and to cleanse us from all unrighteousness" (1 John 1:9). Here's the place to start. Satan gains access to our hearts when we willingly commit sin. Sin originated with lucifer in Heaven. When Adam and Eve sinned, their choice opened a door for the devil to enter humanity. If we want the enemy to leave us, we must lay the axe at the root of the tree (see Matt. 3:10) by confessing and forsaking every habit, practice, or thought pattern we become aware of that is contrary to God's perfect will. The biblical formula is: Sin in, satan in; sin out, satan out. It's that simple. By repenting and turning away from every known sin through the enabling energy of God's grace, we show the Lord we're really serious about permanently leaving the kingdom of darkness. The Bible plainly says, "He who covers his sins will not prosper, But whoever confesses and forsakes *them* will have mercy" (Prov. 28:13).

Defensive Solution #2: Trust Fully in the Blood of Jesus Christ

"This is My blood of the new covenant," Jesus told His disciples the night before His death, "which is shed for many for the remission of sins" (Matt. 26:28). God's last book also testifies of His redeemed: "And they [the saints] overcame him [the devil] by the blood of the Lamb and by the word of their testimony, and they did not love their lives to the death" (Rev. 12:11). None can fully explain it, but the Christian hymn is correct which states:

> Would you be freed from the burden of sin?
> There's power in the blood, power in the blood!
> Would you o'er evil the victory win?
> There's wonderful power in the blood![10]

On Calvary, Jesus Christ shed His blood for us. That blood represents His life, His power—His full authority to forgive every confessed sin. After confessing our sins, we must trust fully, completely, and entirely in the merits of Christ's blood. We aren't worthy, *but Jesus is.* Trusting fully in the "blood of the Lamb" brings forgiveness, special power, and heavenly authority in our battle against evil. Satan and all rebel angels know this, which is why they despise the blood of Jesus Christ. The Bible says we're "redeemed" through "the precious blood of Christ, as of a lamb without blemish and without spot" (1 Pet. 1:18-19). "We have redemption *through His blood*, the forgiveness of sins, according to the riches of His grace" (Eph. 1:7). Devils don't appreciate this.

Defensive Solution #3: Remove All Evil Influences From Your Home

Some are harassed or even tormented by demonic forces inside their own homes. Usually this is because someone has opened a large door for satan through dabbling in witchcraft, playing with Ouija boards, reading occult books, playing games like *Dungeons and Dragons*, watching sinful moves, visiting occult or pornographic web sites, or even through listening to satan-inspired music like heavy metal Rock & Roll. Don't be fooled: Lucifer's legions *work through* every sinful thing contrary to God's perfect will, and if we want our homes free from satanic influences and filled with the love and peace of Heaven, we should banish anything that even smells devilish. David described his behavior in his own house:

> I will behave wisely in a perfect way. Oh, when will You come to me? I will walk within my house with a perfect heart. I will set nothing wicked before my eyes; I hate the work of those who fall away; it shall not cling to me (Psalm 101:2-3).

"Within my house with a perfect heart," David said. "Nothing wicked before my eyes"—this is one key to victory. This not only applies to books, games, and movies directly related to the occult, but to all other sinful magazines, videos, DVDs, and TV shows. Paul's counsel to the Philippians sets the standard for Christian purity and for experiencing "the peace of God" in our homes. Notice carefully:

> *Finally, brethren, whatever things are true, whatever things are noble, whatever things are just, whatever things are pure, whatever things are lovely, whatever things are of good report, if there is any virtue and anything praiseworthy— meditate on these things...**and the God of peace will be with you*** (Philippians 4:8-9).

What happens when we apply this Scripture to J.K. Rowling's *Harry Potter* books? Hopefully, the answer's obvious.

Defensive Solution #4: Put on the Whole Armor of God

Implementing Defensive Solutions 1-3 will drive satan's legions out of our hearts and homes—but we must *keep* them out. If we don't, the unclean spirit may say to itself, "'I will return to my house from which I came.' And when he comes, he finds *it* empty, swept, and put in order. Then he goes and takes with him seven other spirits more wicked than himself, and they enter and dwell there; and the last *state* of that man is worse than the first" (Matt. 12:44-45). Sober thought! When demons exit human bodies, they seek to return. So we must be barricaded for battle. Paul gives this solution:

> *Finally, my brethren, be strong in the Lord and in the power of His might. Put on the whole armor of God, that you may be able to stand against the wiles of the devil. For we do not wrestle against flesh and blood, but against principalities, against powers, against the rulers of the darkness of this age, against spiritual hosts of wickedness in the heavenly places. Therefore take up the whole armor of God, that you may be able to withstand in the evil day, and having done all, to stand. Stand therefore, having girded your waist with truth, having put on the breastplate of righteousness, and having shod your feet with the preparation of the gospel of peace; above all, taking the shield of faith with which you will be*

*able to quench all the fiery darts of the wicked one. And take
the helmet of salvation, and the sword of the Spirit, which is
the word of God; praying always with all prayer and suppli-
cation in the Spirit* (Ephesians 6:10-18).

We need "the whole armor of God," not just part of it. No gaps or
chinks must be allowed—for satan can slip through any crack. "Neither
give place to the devil" (Eph. 4:27 KJV), says the Lord. In our conflict
with principalities and powers, every piece of armor counts. Paul lists
our weaponry as: "truth," "righteousness," "the gospel of peace," "the
shield of faith," "the helmet of salvation," "the sword of the Spirit,
which is the word of God," and "praying always."

Truth: Satan is the father of lies. Error is dangerous. God
longs for us to believe and obey the truth.

Righteousness: We should trust Jesus Christ's righteousness,
not our own. And His righteousness should permeate our actions, not just our profession. By God's grace, we should *do*
right.

The Gospel of Peace: We must know our salvation comes
through what Jesus Christ accomplished by His death and
resurrection. We should also have a peaceful attitude toward
others, as far as possible.

The Shield of Faith: Faith in God is our shield; resist doubt
and unbelief. Trust Christ's protecting power instead of mere
human strength.

The Helmet of Salvation: We must personally believe Jesus
Christ is our Savior. Say, "He loves and died for *me*."

The Sword of the Spirit, which is the Word of God: The Bible
is the Holy Spirit's Book. Through Scripture, the Spirit slash-
es through and exposes error. Truth cuts and often hurts. But
it heals and will save our souls.

Praying Always: We should pray every day, not just in church.
Prayer connects us with the living God. When darkness

comes, pray through it, agonize if need be, and trust the Lord. He promises to send His light.

Defensive Solution #5: Surround Yourself with Strong Christian Friends

This last line of defense is vital. Lions catch their prey by separating them from the herd—then they close in for the kill. Satan does the same thing. He knows that if he can isolate us from other believers it will be easier to overcome us with his temptations, discourage us, and maybe even lead us "to depart from the faith" (1 Tim. 4:1). That's why it's important to surround ourselves with a wholesome network of balanced, spiritually minded, Bible-believing Christian friends.

John wrote, "If we walk in the light, as He is in the light, we have fellowship with one another..." (1 John 1:7). John didn't say "I" but "we." "We" are to "walk in the light" with others who are dwelling in the light. Then we will have "fellowship with one another." If we hang around people who are in the light, it's easier to remain in the light. But if our closest friends are enshrouded in darkness, their darkness will rub off on us—or worse, invade us. Someone wisely said, "Love those best that love Christ most." While we should associate with and seek to influence unbelievers toward faith in the Man With Scars, our closest friends should be other Christians whose influence will encourage, strengthen, and aid us on our journey along the narrow way toward the Celestial City.

Paul also urged, "Not forsaking the assembling of ourselves together, as *is* the manner of some, but exhorting *one another*, and so much the more, as you see the Day approaching" (Heb. 10:25). Some witchcraft books provide guidance for solitary witches, but we shouldn't be solitary Christians. We should meet often with other believers, especially with those who "see the Day approaching," that is, who discern the nearness of Jesus Christ's return. The last two verses in the Bible declare:

He who testifies to these things says, "Surely I am coming quickly." Amen. **Even so, come Lord Jesus!** *The grace of our Lord Jesus Christ be with you all. Amen"* (Revelation 22:20-21).

Much more could be said, but these are the essentials of true "Defense Against the Dark Arts": *forsaking our sins, trusting the blood of Jesus Christ, getting rid of evil things from our homes, putting on the whole armor of God, praying a lot,* and *sticking close to godly friends.* If Harry Potter quit listening to Albus Dumbledore and followed this biblical advice, he'd snap his wand, drop out of Hogwarts, and find new friends—unless he somehow could lead Ron Weasley and Hermione Granger to the foot of the Cross. Who knows? They all might transfer to Bible college and prepare for Christian service.

Seriously, the ones who really need to kneel at Jesus Christ's wounded feet are J.K. Rowling, Silver Ravenwolf, Scott Cunningham, and everyone else who is perhaps unknowingly leading others astray— not from "the Lord and Lady," but from God and the Bible. They don't realize it, but Jesus loves and died for them, too. There's nothing He wants more than to make *witches into Christians.* Don't forget this. The truth is—we all need the Savior, His forgiveness, and His love.

In conclusion: The battle which began in Heaven is now raging between the Creator and lucifer, between Jesus Christ and the devil, between the Holy Spirit and rebel angels, between God's truth and man's errors. Whose side are we on? Are we wearing "the whole armor of God" so we can "stand against the wiles of the devil"? Or are we utterly defenseless, trusting only in the weakness of self?

Without God's full armor, we're no match for satan's forces. But we must always remember that although lucifer is stronger than we are, he's no match for the Almighty. The Lord can oust him with his pinky. God kicked His adversary out of Heaven; and someday soon, He'll crush satan's inexcusable rebellion against His legitimate sovereignty. The Bible's promise is that "we are more than conquerors through Him that loved us" (Rom. 8:37). Hallelujah!

God's last book warns that through *"sorcery* all the nations were deceived" (Rev. 18:23). This is a real prophecy about real sorcery deceiving real nations at the end of time.

In the penetrating light of this non-fiction prediction, I urge you to trust your Creator, to believe in Jesus Christ's love, and to follow the Bible. If you do, you'll avoid the seductive spells of he-who-should-be-named, whom Revelation predicts will ensnare all nations.

You'll enjoy eternity with the Man With Scars.

I hope to see you there.

ENDNOTES

1. Rowling, *Sorcerer's Stone*, pp. 134-135.

2. Rowling, *Order of the Phoenix*, pp. 339-340.

3. Ravenwolf, *Teen Witch*, p. 133.

4. Ravenwolf, *Teen Witch*, pp. 207-208.

5. Vincent McCann, *Set Free From Witchcraft and the Occult. My Story* (Spotlight Ministries, 1998). Available at http://www.spotlight ministries.org.uk/testi.htm.

6. *Ibid.*

7. *Ibid.*

8. *Ibid.*

9. To read the testimonies of those delivered from witchcraft and the occult, see these web sites: Ex Witch Ministries (http://www. exwitch.org), SpotLight Ministries (http://www.spotlightministries. org.uk/stories.htm), Fill the Void (http://www.fillthevoid.org/Wicca/ wicca-witchcraft.html), Berean Faith (http://www.bereanfaith.com/ testimonies.php?action=story&id=108).

10. Lewis E. Jones (1865-1936), song entitled "Power in the Blood," 1899.

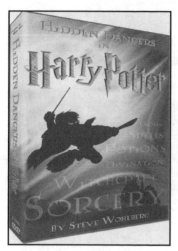

The Antichrist Chronicles
Twelve half-hour programs entirely on the mysterious topic of Antichrist. Explains what the Bible says and what all major Protestant Reformers taught in contrast to modern speculation. Stunning, original graphics. Filmed for television. (Book/Audio/Video/DVD)

Israel in Prophecy
A Jewish believer himself, Steve Wohlberg explains the difference between "Israel after the flesh" (1 Corinthians 10:18) and "the Israel of God" in Jesus Christ (Galatians 6:14-16). Clarifies what the Book of Revelation really teaches about Israel, the temple, Babylon the Great, and Armageddon. (Book/Audio/Video/DVD)

Will My Pet Go to Heaven?

Steve Wohlberg's popular, heart-touching book for pet lovers, tells the tragic story of the death of the Wohlberg's dog, Jax, and Steve's search into the Bible to see what it says about animals. You'll be amazed at what he found! Shares Jesus Christ with those who may not read the Bible, but who love their dog, cat, or horse. A great gift for anyone who has lost a pet.
(Book/Tract)

Additional copies of this book and other
book titles from DESTINY IMAGE are
available at your local bookstore.

For a bookstore near you, call 1-800-722-6774.

Send a request for a catalog to:

Destiny Image® Publishers, Inc.
P.O. Box 310
Shippensburg, PA 17257-0310

*"Speaking to the Purposes of God for This
Generation and for the Generations to Come"*

For a complete list of our titles,
visit us at www.destinyimage.com